Maths and Stats fo Web Analytics and Conversion Optimization

Written by Himanshu Sharma, Founder of Optimize Smart

Maths and Stats for Web Analytics and Conversion Optimization
Written by Himanshu Sharma, Founder of Optimize Smart

*This book is dedicated to my wonderful wife Helen
and the most awesome Pug in the world 'Mooli'.*

Table of contents

About the author

Himanshu Sharma is the founder of Optimize Smart, a UK based digital marketing consultancy which specializes in analytics consultation and conversion optimization.

Himanshu has more than ten years' experience in SEO, PPC and web analytics. He holds a bachelors' degree in 'Internet Science' and is a certified web analyst.

He was nominated for a Digital Analytics Association award for excellence. The Digital Analytics Association is a world renowned not-for-profit association which helps organizations overcome the challenges of data acquisition and application.

Himanshu runs a popular blog on OptimizeSmart.com which has more than 10,000 subscribers and gets more than a quarter of a million visits a month from over 100 countries.

Follow him on twitter: @analyticsnerd

Introduction

The role of maths and statistics in the world of web analytics is not clear to many marketers. Not many talk or write about the usage of statistics and data science in conversion optimization. This book has been written to fill this knowledge gap.

Often big heavy books on maths and statistics teach you more than you need to know, you learn things that you may never use in your working life. Not only do such books waste your time and money but they also constantly push you to give up on learning key maths and statistics skills.

This expert guide will teach you exactly what you need to know. It will teach you how to leverage the knowledge of maths and statistics in order to accurately interpret data and take actions which can quickly improve the bottom-line of your online business.

Every topic that I have covered in this book has something to do directly with your day to day job. This is not a book that will help you to become a fully-fledged statistician or a book to be used to pass your maths/statistics college exam.

This book covers vital topics on maths and statistics which every internet marketer/web analyst should get familiar with in order to achieve optimum results from their analysis, marketing campaigns and conversion optimization efforts.

I will explain some of the most useful statistics terms/concepts one by one and will also show you their practical use in web analytics and conversion optimization, so that you can take advantage of them straightaway.

Why do you need to know the maths and stats behind web analytics and conversion optimization?

It is not just about what you should know, it is about what you are expected to know, especially if you deal with businesses day in, day out.

Here are few questions for your consideration:

Q1. When your website conversion rate jumps from 10% to 12%, is this a 2% rise in conversion rate or a 20% rise in conversion rate?

Q2. Can you double your sales by simply doubling your marketing budget?

Q3. Should you focus on a large number of low value customers or focus on a few high value customers to maximize profit?

Q4. If the conversion rate of campaign A is 10% and the conversion rate of campaign B conversion is 20%, does that mean campaign B is performing better than campaign A?

Q5. The average time on your website is five minutes. Does that mean website visitors actually spend five minutes on average?

I am sure many marketers/analysts will make mistakes while answering these questions. I am sure because I made these mistakes too. I was not born with statistical knowledge. It is something which I acquired over time and I am still acquiring.

So if you are not sure about the answers to my questions than this is perfectly normal.

However, if I happen to be your client or boss then it is not normal. Sorry. You have disappointed me and I now doubt your reports.

Consultant: Boss, conversion rate has improved by 2% in the last four months. Four months ago it was 10%, now it is 12%.

Boss: You have made a complete mess of the figures. Sales are at an all-time low. Off you go! Grrr!

The grumpy boss may not know that there has been a negative correlation between conversion rate and revenue and there is no 2% rise in conversion rate.

But what he does know for sure is that sales are going down and that he is less profitable. Now he has a moral obligation to do the dreaded 'cost cutting'.

Guess whose job is on the line next?

The corporate world is not very forgiving of mistakes made by employees/consultants/ agencies. So if we report that the jump in conversion rate from 10% to 12% means there is a 2% rise in conversion rate, our entire marketing report becomes questionable.

We instantly create a shadow on the rest of our analysis. The thought that will instantly pop into the mind of the recipient of our report will be "what else has he done wrong?"

Learning maths and statistics is an excellent way to develop your logical and critical thinking. It makes you a better marketer and, of course, a better analyst

Then no one can easily question your reasoning skills and you become a true NINJA.

Part one:

The maths for web analytics and conversion optimization

Lesson 1: An introduction to return on investment (ROI)

Return on investment (ROI) is used to evaluate the efficiency of your investment and/or to compare the efficiency of different investments.

> *Return on investment*
> *= (gain from investment – cost of investment) / cost of investment*

We often talk about ROI during reporting and especially during a pitch to a new client.

> *"ROI is a very important metric, even more important than sales or conversions."*

This is because ROI takes into account the **cost of the investment**.

Common business sense dictates that if an investment does not yield a positive ROI, or if there are other marketing channels with a higher ROI, then the investment from a particular marketing channel should be withdrawn.

Types of ROI in online marketing

In the world of online marketing there can be three types of ROI:

1. Anticipated ROI

2. Immediate ROI

3. Actual ROI

Anticipated ROI

Anticipated ROI

= (anticipated revenue from your marketing campaigns – proposed cost of your marketing campaigns) / proposed cost of your marketing campaigns

Anticipated ROI is the ROI we forecast when we are pitching to a new client.

Immediate ROI

Immediate ROI

= (total revenue from your marketing campaigns – total cost of your marketing campaigns) / total cost of your marketing campaigns

Immediate ROI is the ROI we get when we run marketing campaigns.

Actual ROI

Actual ROI

*= Immediate ROI * 12*

Actual ROI is based on long term benefits and the fact that a client continues to get returns from your conversion optimization efforts for a long period of time (at least 12 months) after you have stopped optimized his website/campaigns for conversions.

Actual ROI calculations can take 'customer life time value' into account.

1. **0% ROI** means no profit, no loss. You spent X and earned X in revenue.
2. **100% ROI** means you spent X and earned 2X in revenue.
3. **1000% ROI** means you spent X and earned 11X in revenue.
4. **-100% ROI** means you spent X and earned 0 in revenue.

I think it is pretty reasonable to consider delivering at least 100% ROI.

If your client spends X and earns X in return, then he is not going to make any money. If he spends X and earns less than X in return then he is losing money.

Lesson 2: ROI analysis in Google Analytics

Requirements for ROI analysis in Google Analytics

There are four primary requirements to calculate the ROI of various marketing campaigns in Google Analytics:

1. Availability of **website usage** data in your analytics reports.
2. Availability of **ecommerce** data in your analytics reports.
3. Availability of **goal conversions** data in your analytics reports.
4. Availability of **cost** data in your analytics reports.

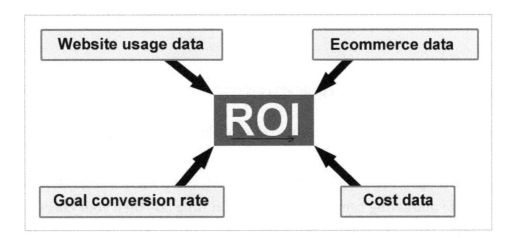

Unless you have all of this data in place, you cannot accurately calculate the ROI of your marketing campaigns.

This is because Google Analytics calculates ROI as:

Return on investment
= (total ecommerce revenue + total goal value − cost) / cost

To get website usage data, such as sessions, bounce rate etc., you simply need to set up a Google Analytics account.

To get ecommerce data (such as revenue) in your reports, you need to set up ecommerce tracking.

To get goal conversions data (such as the economic value of your newsletter signups) in your reports you need to set up conversion tracking.

Make sure that each goal you have set up has the correct **goal value**.

A goal conversion without a goal value is an empty conversion.

To get cost data in your analytics reports, you need to either manually upload cost data into your Google Analytics view or you can use the Management API to automate this process.

An introduction to cost data

The cost data is simply the cost of running your marketing campaigns.

For example, if you spend £3,500 per month on SEO, £1,500 per month on Facebook, £1,500 on affiliate marketing campaigns, £2,000 on Bing ads then your cost data can be represented by the following table:

Campaign	Cost
SEO	£3,500
Facebook	£1,500
Affiliates	£1,500
Bing ads	£2,000

You need to upload this cost data into your Google Analytics (GA) view so that GA can calculate the ROI of these marketing channels.

> *"If you do not have cost data available in your Google Analytics reports then you cannot calculate the ROI of various marketing campaigns."*

There are two methods available for uploading cost data in Google Analytics:

1. By creating a **data set** through the 'data import' menu.
2. By creating **custom data sources** through the 'custom definitions' menu.

Google recommends uploading cost data through the 'data import' menu instead of custom data sources because custom data sources are likely to be depreciated in the coming months.

An introduction to data sets

> *"A data set is simply a container that holds the data you want to upload to Google Analytics."*

Each container has been designed to hold only a specific type of data. This data can be cost data, user data, product data, content data, custom data etc.

Consequently we can have different types of data sets in GA:

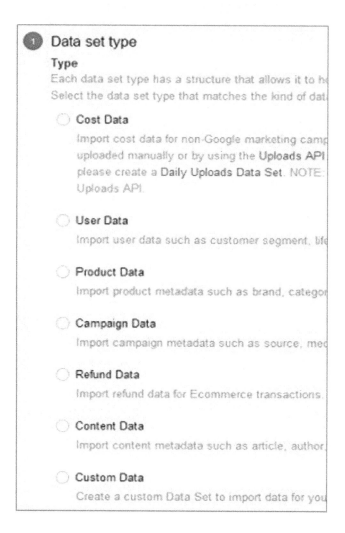

So if you want to store cost data then you need to create a data set which can hold cost data. Similarly, if you want to store user data then you need to create a data set which can hold user data.

Note: You cannot store cost data in a data set meant for another purpose, such as storing user data. If you want to store cost data then you need to create a data set which can hold such type of data.

An introduction to data set schemas

When you create a data set, you need to define the schema of the data set. A schema is simply the structure/format in which you will upload data to Google Analytics.

For example Google Analytics uses the 'ga:source' schema to identify the campaign source, the 'ga:medium' schema to identify the campaign medium and the ga:keyword to identify keywords and so on.

Following is the schema I have defined for uploading Bing ads cost data in Google Analytics:

Once you have defined your cost data schema/format, you then need to format your Bing ads cost data according to this schema. Otherwise, you will get errors after the upload.

Following is an example of Bing ads cost data, first in unformatted form and then in formatted form (i.e. according to the pre-defined schema):

Unformatted Bing Ads Cost Data								
Date	Source	Medium	Campaigns	Ad group	Keyword	Impressions	Clicks	Cost
04/08/2014 Bing		cpc	Tops	Crop tops	crop top	45	12	3.24
04/08/2014 Bing		cpc	Tops	Crop tops	crop top pattern	533	342	11.3
04/08/2014 Bing		cpc	Tops	Crop tops	crop top bathing suit	3554	1235	56.74

Formatted Bing Ads Cost Data								
ga:date	ga:source	ga:medium	ga:campaign	ga:adGroup	ga:keyword	ga:impressions	ga:adClicks	ga:adCost
20140804 Bing		CPC	Tops	Crop tops	crop top	45	12	3.24
20140804 Bing		CPC	Tops	Crop tops	crop top pattern	533	342	11.3
20140804 Bing		CPC	Tops	Crop tops	crop top bathing suit	3554	1235	56.74

As you can see from the screenshot, the formatting of the cost data is not that hard.

Similarly, following is the schema I have defined for uploading Facebook ads cost data in Google Analytics:

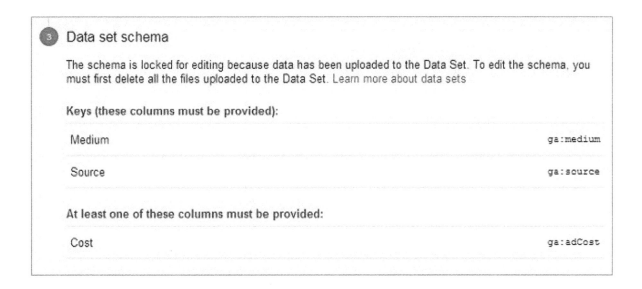

Note: You do not have to follow my schemas. You can upload cost data in any format you want as long as the format is supported by Google Analytics and as long as the format matches with the data set schema you defined while creating the cost data set.

Once you have defined your cost data schema/format, you then need to format your Facebook ads cost data according to this schema.

Following is an example of Facebook ads cost data, first in unformatted form and then in formatted form (i.e. according to pre-defined schema):

Unformatted Facebook Cost Data

Date	Total Ad cost
August 1, 2014	£321.00
August 2, 2014	£127.00
August 3, 2014	£243.00
August 4, 2014	£541.00
August 5, 2014	£234.00
August 6, 2014	£432.00

Formatted Facebook Cost Data

ga:date	ga:medium	ga:source	ga:adCost
20140801	social	Facebook-Ads	321
20140802	social	Facebook-Ads	127
20140803	social	Facebook-Ads	243
20140804	social	Facebook-Ads	541
20140805	social	Facebook-Ads	234
20140806	social	Facebook-Ads	432

Importing cost data into Google Analytics via data sets

Follow the steps below to import cost data via data sets:

Step 1. Tag all of your marketing campaigns.

Step 2. Collect cost data.

Step 3. Create data set and define data set schema.

Step 4. Format your cost data.

Step 5. Upload the cost data.

Step 1. Tag all of your marketing campaigns

Make sure that all of your non-google marketing campaigns (like Facebook ads, Bing ads, email campaigns, affiliate campaigns etc.) have got campaign tracking parameters (utm_source, utm_medium, utm_campaign, utm_term, and utm_content).

Campaign tracking parameters are required in order to tie website usage data (such as sessions), goals data (such as newsletters signups) and ecommerce data (such as revenue) to the correct marketing campaign.

Step 2. Collect cost data

You need to determine the cost data of all the non-google marketing campaigns you are currently tracking. I generally collect/download one month of cost data for each marketing campaign in the first week of the following month.

For example, on 1st August, I collected all of the July cost data (not in aggregate form) for each marketing campaign and then uploaded all of the data in one go. Google Analytics lets you upload historical data and can calculate ROI retroactively. You can also upload cost data every day for each of your campaigns. But I do not do that. Not at least manually.

Step 3. Create the data set and define the data set schema

3.1   Click on the 'admin' link at the top right hand side in your GA account.

3.2   Select the property for which you want to create the data set.

3.3   Under the property section, click on the 'data import' menu:

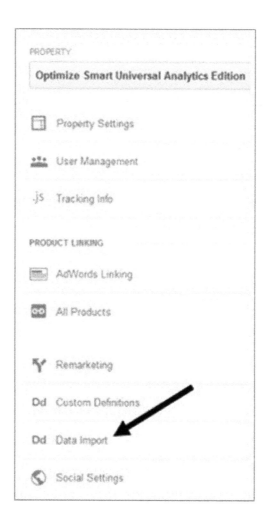

3.4 Click on '+ new data set' button. Then select 'cost data' as the data set type and then click on the 'next step' button.

3.5 Name you data set and select the view(s) that will use the cost data:

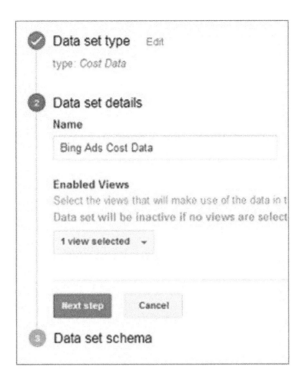

3.6 In the next step you need to define your data set schema:

You can define the data set schema, like I did above, for uploading Bing ads or you can choose your own format.

3.7 Keep the 'import behavior' settings to 'summation' unless you want to overwrite the old cost data. Now click on the 'save' button.

3.8 Once you clicked on the 'save' button, you will see two more buttons: 'get schema' and 'get custom data source ID (for API users)':

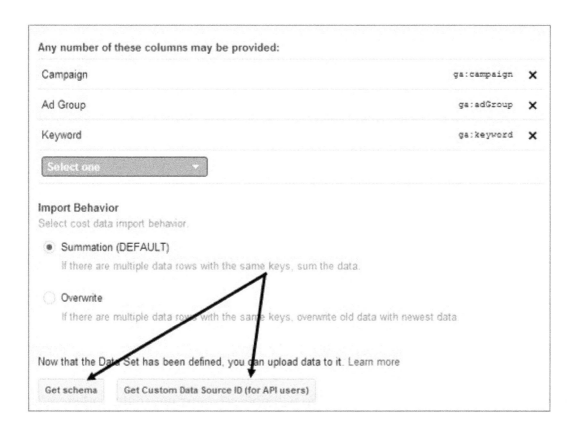

3.9 Click on the 'get schema' button and then download the schema template (which is a CSV file) by clicking on the 'download schema template' button:

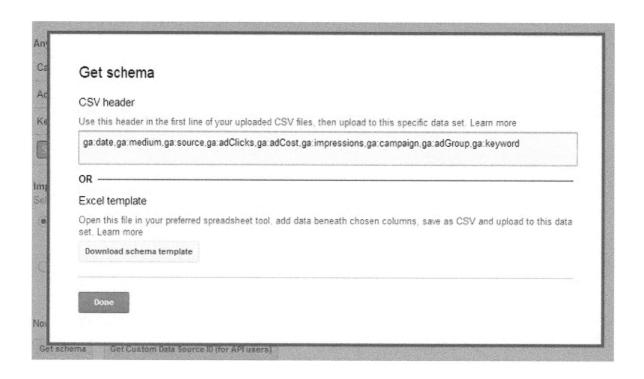

3.10 Click on the 'done' button twice. You will now see your new data set listed on the data set table:

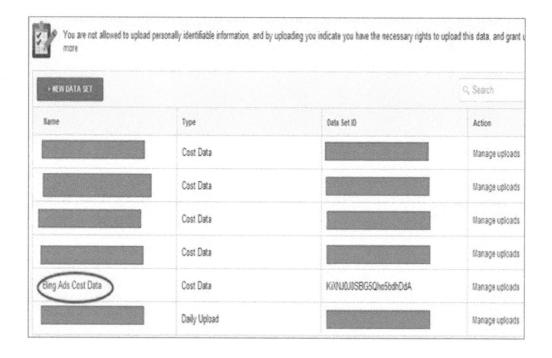

"You should create one cost data set for each external data source whose cost data you want to import into Google Analytics."

Following is the visual summary of cost data sets:

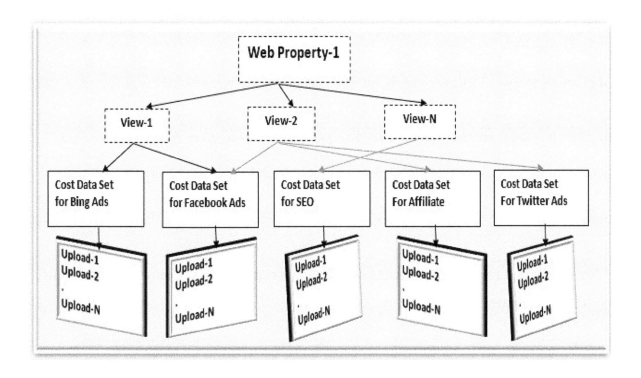

Create one cost data set for Bing ads, one for affiliate websites, one for Facebook campaigns and one for each campaign you are currently tracking.

When you create different cost data sets for different external data sources, it becomes easier to manage cost data among different views.

If you create a single cost data set for both Bing ads and Facebook ads then later you want to delete the Bing ads cost data, it would also delete the Facebook cost data from your view reports.

So the best practice is to create one cost data set for each external data source.

Step 4. Format your cost data

4.1 Open the schema template you downloaded, in Excel:

4.2 Now you need to add and format your Bing ads cost data according to the schema defined in the template:

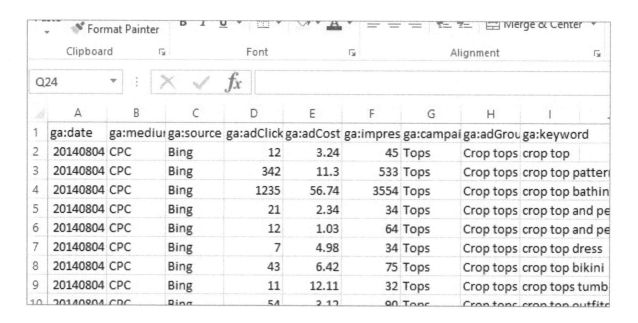

4.3   Once you have finished formatting the data, rename your schema template file and make sure you save the schema template file as a CSV file. Your file is now ready to be uploaded to Google Analytics.

Step 5. Upload the cost data

5.1   Click on the 'manage uploads' link in the data set table:

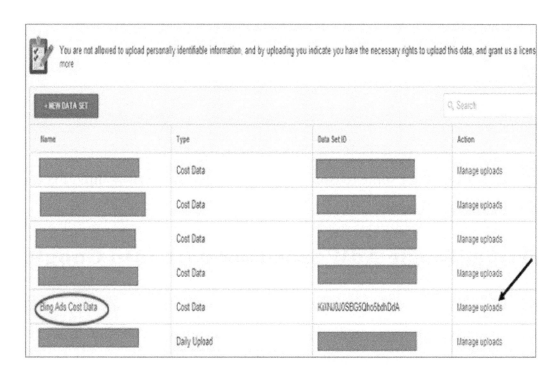

5.2   Click on the 'upload file' button and then upload your Bing ads cost data file.

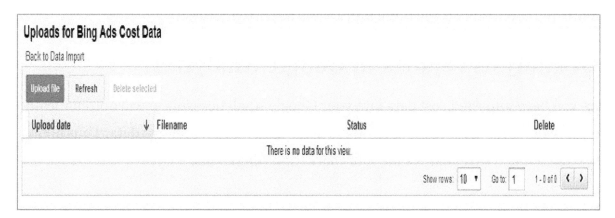

If your upload is successful you will see a 'completed' status, otherwise you will see a 'failed' status:

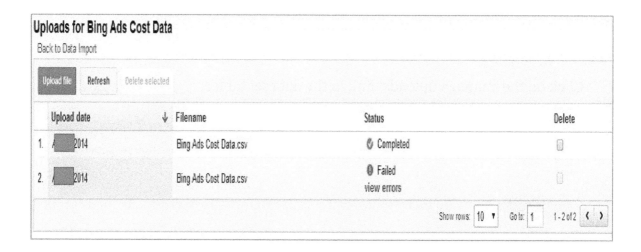

If your upload has failed for some reason then click on the 'view errors' link. Fix the errors and then upload your file again.

Importing Google AdWords cost data into Google Analytics

In the case of Google AdWords you do not need to go through all the trouble of creating a cost data set and retrieving and formatting cost data.

All you have to do is to link your Google AdWords account to your Google Analytics account and the cost data will automatically be imported into GA.

ROI analysis reports in Google Analytics

Once you have imported cost data into your Google Analytics view, it will automatically get integrated with the website usage data, goals data and ecommerce data. Thus allowing you to do detailed ROI analysis for your marketing campaigns.

You can then see the imported cost data in the following reports:

1. Cost analysis report (under the 'acquisition' menu).
2. Custom report which includes cost and ROI data.
3. ROI analysis report (under 'conversions', then the 'attribution' menu).

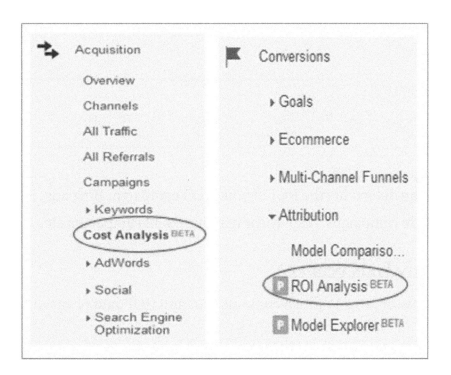

Cost analysis report

Through the cost analysis report you can determine the cost per click, ROI and margin of all of the marketing channels whose cost data you have imported into Google Analytics view.

This means you can determine the ROI of your SEO campaign, Bing ads, Facebook campaigns, affiliate campaigns, display campaigns, email campaigns etc.

Custom cost analysis report

Following is the custom report which contains cost and ROI data of various campaigns:

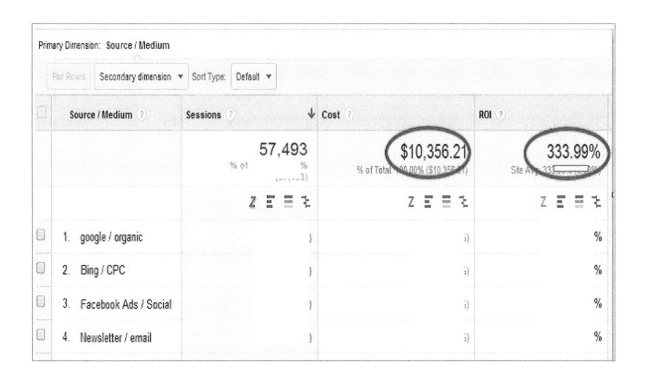

ROI analysis report

The downside of the cost analysis report is that all of the ROI data is calculated using only one attribution model called 'last non-direct click'.

If you want to do ROI analysis using the attribution model which is most appropriate for your business then you need to use the ROI analysis report:

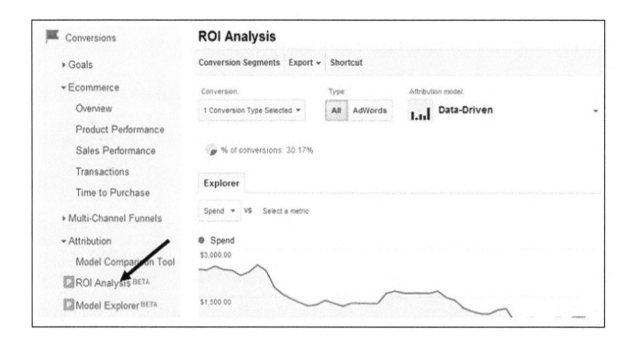

Through the ROI analysis report you can determine **cost per acquisition (CPA)** and **return on advertising spend (ROAS)** under different attribution models.

So instead of just the regular CPA, you can actually determine:

1. Last interaction CPA.
2. Last non-direct click CPA.
3. Last AdWords click CPA.
4. First interaction CPA.
5. Linear CPA.
6. Time decay CPA.
7. Position based CPA.
8. Data driven CPA.
9. CPA based on any custom attribution model.

Similarly, you can determine

1. Last interaction ROAS.
2. Last non-direct click ROAS.
3. Last AdWords click ROAS.
4. First interaction ROAS.
5. Linear ROAS.
6. Time decay ROAS.
7. Position based ROAS.
8. Data driven ROAS.
9. ROAS based on any custom attribution model.

Lesson 3: Conversions and ROI in a multi-channel marketing world

When we talk about attribution modelling and multi-channel marketing, we do not say 'conversions'. We say something like 'last click conversions', 'first click conversions or 'data driven conversions'.

That is how Google Analytics reports conversions and that is how conversions should be reported.

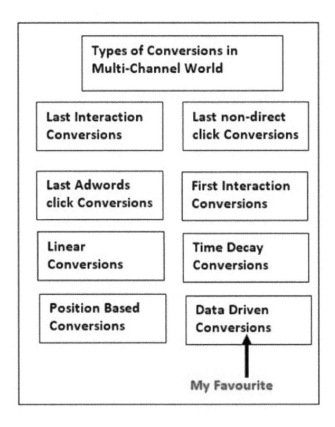

There are around eight different types of conversions available in Google Analytics reports and one different conversion type for each custom attribution model.

When you look at your marketing from this perspective, it completely changes the way you interpret and report ROI.

Lesson 4: ROI calculations for SEO

It is not easy to calculate the ROI of SEO campaigns.

If a business does not see any apparent ROI from SEO, or finds other marketing channels more lucrative in terms of ROI, than it may either choose to cut down the SEO budget or stop the SEO campaign altogether and invest the money somewhere else.

This can happen in companies which run multi-channel marketing, where SEO is not playing a very big role in revenue generation or where the SEO has failed to prove the ROI of its efforts.

Therefore it becomes very important that we calculate and report the ROI of our SEO campaign even if the client has not asked for it. This is because if we do not report the ROI, the client will calculate it himself (often inaccurately) at some point - especially during the decision whether to continue or discontinue SEO.

Every time we report ROI, we give a solid reason to our client why they should continue to invest in SEO.

> *"For clients, ROI always means 'dollar returns'.*
>
> *ROI should not be confused with raw organic traffic, organic conversions, rankings, number of links built etc. The majority of businesses cannot understand ROI in these terms. They want to know if they spend X, then what are they going to get in return in dollar value. Is it 2X, 3X...?"*

You need to report the ROI for the sake of your business.

Types of SEO ROI

There are three types of SEO ROI:

1. Anticipated SEO ROI.
2. Immediate SEO ROI.
3. Actual SEO ROI.

Anticipated SEO ROI

> *Anticipated SEO ROI*
> *= (anticipated revenue from SEO efforts – proposed cost of the SEO project) / proposed cost of the SEO project (measured in percentage)*

Before you calculate anticipated ROI, you need to know three things in advance from your prospective client:

1. Average monthly visits (or sessions).
2. Ecommerce conversion rate of the website.
3. Average order value.

If you do not have these values beforehand than you cannot do 'anticipated ROI' calculations.

Let us suppose that you have got following data from your prospective client:

1. Average monthly visits – 50,000.
2. Ecommerce conversion rate of the website – 0.68%.
3. Average order value – $176.

Let us suppose that the proposed cost (or fee) of your SEO project is $20,000. Now you need to justify this spend to your prospective client.

So you need to generate an additional sale of at least $20k during your contract period. But $20k will only be a break-even point (point at which there is no profit and no loss) for your client.

So you need to generate much more than $20k through your SEO efforts in order to generate a **reasonably positive ROI**.

You now need to determine the number of additional orders required to generate an additional sale of at least $20k on the client website:

No. of additional orders required for $20k sale
= proposed sale/average order value
= 20000/176
= 114

So when you have generated an additional 114 orders on the client's website during your contract period through your SEO efforts, your client will break-even.

If you fail to generate at least 114 orders through your SEO efforts during your contract term than you will generate a negative ROI for your client. Your client will actually be in a loss.

The next thing that you need to do is determine the additional traffic required to generate 114 orders on the client's website:

Additional traffic required to break even
= number of orders required to break-even / ecommerce conversion rate

= 114/0.68%

= 16,765 visits

Therefore you need to generate at least 16,765 visits to the website through organic search just to break-even.

Here I am assuming that the ecommerce conversion rate of the website will remain constant (if not improved) during the contract term.

In order to deliver a **reasonably positive ROI**, you need to generate much more than 16,765 visits.

So let us just double this traffic estimate to 33,530 visits (16765 * 2). Now we can expect to get around 228 orders (144 * 2) through our SEO efforts, which in turn could result in $40k ($20 * 2) in sales.

Anticipated ROI
= (anticipated revenue from SEO efforts – proposed cost of the SEO project) / proposed cost of the SEO project
= ($40,000 – $20,000) / $20,000
= 100%

100% ROI means if your client spend X, he earns 2X in return.

I think it is pretty reasonable to consider delivering at least this much ROI. If your client spends X and earns X or less in return, then what is the point of carrying out SEO on the website in the first place. It is simply a waste of time and money.

Now at this stage you need to decide whether or not you can generate an additional 33,530 visits through SEO during your proposed time frame.

You can do this by estimating the traffic you could generate through your chosen keywords in the proposed time frame.

You can always go back and revise your proposed fees and time frame for the project if you think 33k visits is too much to deliver.

Once you have done your traffic projections and ROI calculation then it is up to the client to decide whether he can trust you on your ability to generate the proposed traffic to his website within the timeframe.

In any case, you now know how the 'anticipated ROI' calculation is carried out and why it is so important.

When you talk about ROI, you should always speak in a language which businesses understand very well:

> *"Ok I will give you X, how much will I get in return?... Please do not tell me I will get rankings and traffic in return. Tell me how much I will get in dollar value so that I can justify ad spend."*

Immediate SEO ROI

> *Immediate SEO ROI*
> *= (total ecommerce revenue through SEO + total goal value of assisted conversions through SEO – total cost of running the SEO campaign) / total cost of running the SEO campaign (measured in percentage)*

Immediate ROI is the ROI you get when you start running SEO campaigns. This is the ROI which eventually decides the fate of your future engagement with a client.

I calculate 'total goal value through SEO' as the sum of the value of various assisting conversions. I am taking multi touch attribution into account here because:

"SEO not only helps in completing a conversion but also helps in initiating and assisting the conversions which are completed by other marketing channels (such as PPC, email, display, direct, referral etc.)"

So you must report the role of organic search campaigns in the overall conversions occurred on the website. SEO takes a long time to show positive ROI. So it is best to report ROI after four to six months of starting the campaigns.

Let's assume that:

- The total ecommerce revenue through SEO in the last six months was $50,000.
- The total goal value of assisted conversions through SEO in the last four months was $10,000 (you can determine assisted conversions value through the 'assisted conversions' report in Google Analytics).
- The total cost of running the SEO campaign in the last six months was $12,000.

The calculation for immediate ROI would be:

Immediate ROI
= ($50,000 + $10,000 - $12000) / $12000
= 400%

Actual SEO ROI

Actual SEO ROI
= immediate ROI*12 (measured in percentage)

The client will continue to get SEO benefits at least for the next one year even without any SEO.

Actual SEO ROI
= immediate ROI*12

= 400%*12

= 4800%

Remember whatever you charge as your SEO fees for the total duration of the project is the total cost of running the SEO campaign for your client.

So in order to generate a reasonably positive ROI (100%), you need to generate an additional sales for your client through SEO which is at least twice as much as your SEO fees.

If you generate sales which are less than your total SEO fees, then your client will get a negative return on his investment. If you generate as much sales revenue as your total SEO fees, then your client will get 0% return on his investment.

In order to generate a reasonably positive ROI (such as 100% ROI or more), you must generate sales which are at least twice the amount of your total SEO fees. So if you are charging $10k for the total duration of the SEO project, then your proposed additional sale through SEO would be $10k * 2 = $20k

> *"Remember, the real magic is in what you report. If you have got it, flaunt it! It is critical that you show the value of your SEO efforts. Never blindly assume that the client already knows about your great work"*

I am able to prove to a business that if they cut costs on SEO, it will impact their PPC, display, social media and email campaigns. I expect the same from you.

When is the best time to report SEO ROI?

I am often asked this question. The best time to report the ROI of your SEO campaign is when you start getting positive ROI.

> *"Never report negative ROI."*

It is common for SEO campaigns to show negative ROI for the first few months and this is something you can warn your client about in advance.

Once you start getting positive ROI, no matter how small, just report it. Even 10% positive ROI is worth reporting.

Lesson 5: ROI calculations for phone call tracking

I love phone call tracking simply because it gives me a break from the regular tracking I do using Google Analytics and other similar tools. If you have been in the field of digital marketing as long as I have (almost a decade), you tend to get a bit bored of looking at the same metrics over and over again.

This is not really the case with phone call tracking as it comes with a whole new set of metrics and a cool reporting interface where you get the chance to optimize an entirely different marketing channel called 'phone'.

I have developed my own simple Step by-step process to achieve ROI calculations for phone call tracking:

Step 1: Selling the concept of phone call tracking to your client/boss.

Step 2: Setting up phone call tracking.

Step 3: Setting up phone calls as goal conversions in Google Analytics.

Step 4: Training call centre staff to make notes and score each phone call.

Step 5: Entering your ad spend for each marketing channel and calculating ROI.

Step 6: Determining the performance of your call centre staff.

Step 7: Creating custom reports for detailed phone call analysis in Google Analytics.

Step 1. Selling the concept of phone call tracking to your client/boss

Many companies are still not familiar with the concept of phone call tracking and they will not use it until you as a marketer/analyst can convince them that it is worth the investment.

In order to sell phone call tracking you need to do two things:

1. Explain the benefits of phone call tracking.
2. Explain how phone call tracking works.

Benefits of phone call tracking

1. Attribute phone calls to the correct traffic source

If your website has been set up mainly to generate leads through phone calls (this is quite common for websites which sell high priced items such as property, cars, yachts, consultation services etc.) then you have to attribute phone calls to the correct traffic source in order to **prove** the value that you have added to the business bottom-line through various marketing channels (SEO, PPC, email, social media etc.) in **monetary terms.**

Through call tracking software you can determine how many phone calls came from SEO, how many came from PPC, print ads, radio ads, billboard ads, TV ad campaigns etc.

You can determine not only the volume of phone calls from each traffic source but also their **quality** (in terms of generating sales).

"Understanding exactly which marketing channels and keywords are driving phone calls is invaluable."

Attributing phone calls to the correct marketing channels means you can increase the budget of the marketing channels which drive phone calls and reduce the budget of those that do not.

For example, if you are running TV ad campaigns, you can determine both the volume and quality of calls through TV ads and also calculate the ROI via your phone call tracking software.

If the **ROI from TV ads** turns out to be negative, you can then choose to make changes to your TV ads or possibly shut down the whole campaign.

> *"In my experience, TV ads generate low quality leads with a high cost per acquisition. However, I suggest you do your own tests and draw your own conclusions."*

Similarly, attributing phone calls to the correct keywords means you are able to bid more aggressively on the keywords that work and reduce bids on the keywords that do not.

2. Import phone call data into Google Analytics

Any call tracking software worth its salt will let you import phone call data into Google Analytics. If it does not do this then it is not worth getting.

You can attribute phone calls to the correct traffic sources either through the   phone call tracking software or through Google Analytics. However:

> *"Google Analytics cannot track phone calls on its own."*

Before you can do anything with the data in Google Analytics you first need to import the phone call data from a call tracking software into Google Analytics. Therefore getting call tracking software is a must. In any case:

> *"Call tracking software provides more detail about the phone calls than Google Analytics ever will."*

3. Correlate phone call data with website usage data

Once you have imported the phone call data into Google Analytics, you can then correlate the call data with other metrics such as traffic sources, keywords, visits, pageviews etc.

This way you can use phone call data to optimize your online marketing campaign.

4. Fix online and offline attribution issues

If phone calls are an important part of your lead generation process then call tracking is one of the best ways to fix your online and offline attribution issues.

5. Track the performance of call centre staff

It is always a struggle to determine how your call centre staff are performing. Through phone call tracking, you can go one step further and determine the performance of each **Customer Service Representative (CSR)** in terms of calls answered, calls closed and revenue generated.

6. Calculate phone call conversion rate

> *Call conversion rate*
> *= number of phone calls which resulted in a sale / total number of phone calls*

For example, if out of 1,000 calls, 100 phone calls resulted in a sale then phone call conversion rate would be 100/1000 = 0.1%.

Phone call conversion rate is calculated for both inbound and outbound calls.

> *Inbound phone call conversion rate*
> *= number of inbound calls which resulted in a sale / total number of unique inbound calls*

I have used unique calls here because sometime the same caller can call multiple times before they convert and thus can skew the conversion rate.

> *Outbound phone call conversion rate*
> *= number of outbound calls which resulted in a sale / total number of outbound calls*

I have not used unique calls here because every call made by a CSR is a cost to the company and our aim is to generate sales via the lowest possible number of outbound calls.

One of the principal benefits of phone call tracking is that you can drill down one step further in your conversion funnel and determine exactly how many phone calls actually turned into sales.

This will help you in determining the conversion rate of not only your marketing campaigns but also your call centre staff.

7. Evaluate the quality of phone call leads

Through call tracking software you are able to separate **low quality phone calls** (calls which did not result in sales) from **high quality phone calls.** You also have the ability to evaluate the performance of the call centre staff that are handling these calls.

> *"In my experience, the shorter the duration of a phone call, the lower the probability of getting a sale.*
>
> *The longer the duration of a phone call, the higher the probability that the caller will eventually end up making a purchase from you."*

A caller will continue the conversation only if they are really interested in your product/service and/or comfortable talking to your call centre staff.

Very short duration phone calls are often wrong numbers or hang ups.

You can also evaluate low quality phone calls by listening to the conversations between callers and your CSR and determine why the calls did not result in sales and what can be done to improve the **customer's phone call experience**. This way you can convert more phone call leads into sales.

> *"If you focus on getting high quality phone call leads and converting more of these leads into sales, you can dramatically improve your phone call ROI."*

Needless to say:

> *"You can save tens of thousands of dollars by setting up phone call tracking system in your company."*

How phone call tracking works

First of all, I use and recommend Call Tracking Metrics (calltrackingmetrics.com). I have used many call tracking services in the past and this is the best one so far.

Call Tracking Metrics (CTM) is easy to use, provides local/toll free numbers in 30 countries around the world and it integrates well with Google Analytics, Kissmetrics, Optimizely and CRMs like Highrise, Hubspot, Salesforce etc.

Going forward, whenever I talk about a software specific feature, it is going to relate to CTM.

Here is how phone call tracking works in CTM (all call tracking software works in pretty much the same way):

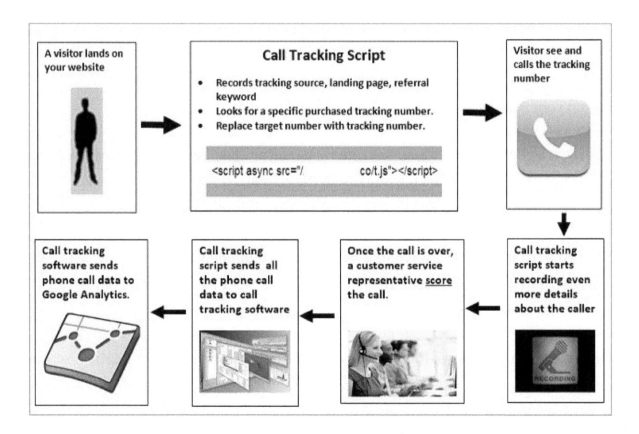

1. As soon as a visitor lands on your website, the call tracking script placed on your website records the tracking source, landing page and the keywords used (if any).

This tracking source can be: direct, Google organic, Google paid, Yahoo organic, Yahoo paid, Bing organic, Bing paid, referral, Facebook, Twitter, YouTube, TV, radio, print etc.

2. The call tracking script looks for the traffic source specific **tracking number** which you bought in your call tracking account. If the script is able to find that number then it replaces the target number (the number that is hard coded on your website) with the tracking number.

For example if a visitor lands on your website via Google organic then he is going to see a Google Organic tracking number instead of the phone number hard coded on your website.

If a visitor lands on your website via Google paid search (Google AdWords) then he is going to see a Google paid tracking number instead of the phone number that is hard coded on your website.

Similarly, if a visitor lands on your website via a referral then he is going to see a referral tracking number, a direct tracking number in the case of a direct visit, a Facebook tracking number in the case of a visit through Facebook, and so on.

3. The visitor calls the tracking number instead of your phone number and the call tracking script starts recording more details about the caller like the actual phone call conversation, phone duration etc.

4. Once the visitor completes the call, the CSR (Customer Service Representative) scores the call (more about this later) using call tracking software.

5. The call tracking script sends all the phone call data to the call tracking software.

6. The call tracking software sends phone call data (only some of the data and not all) to Google Analytics, Kissmetrics etc.

Step 2. Setting up phone call tracking

1. Add phone numbers to your website

While this is normally a no-brainer you now need to be more **strategic** about how you display phone numbers on your website. You need to prominently display phone numbers and remove other Call to Actions (CTA) around the numbers in order to increase the probability of getting phone calls.

2. Purchase tracking numbers

You need to buy at least one tracking number per tracking source in order to track phone calls from a particular source. If you do not do this then you will not be able to track phone calls from a particular traffic source.

For example, if you do not buy a tracking number for direct traffic then you will not be able to track phone calls coming from direct traffic.

Similarly, if you do not buy a tracking number for Google organic then you will not be able to track phone calls coming from Google organic searches.

In real life you need to buy a lot more than just one tracking number for each traffic source.

Call Tracking Metrics (CTM) uses a metric called **likelihood score** (also known as accuracy score) which refers to how confident CTM is that a particular website visitor made a particular phone call.

The score can range from 1% to 100%, with 100% being the most confident.

In order to keep your likelihood scores as close to 100% as possible, CTM recommends buying one tracking number for every forty daily visitors to your website from a particular traffic source.

So if you wish to keep your likelihood scores as close to 100% as possible (which you should) for a particular traffic source then you need to buy tracking numbers equal to your **daily** visitors from the traffic source / 40.

For example, if you want to keep your likelihood scores as close to 100% as possible for say 'Google organic search' and you are getting say 30,000 **monthly** visitors through organic search, then the number of tracking numbers you need to buy would be:

(30000/30) / 40 = 25.

So you would need to buy 25 tracking numbers just for Google organic search. Needless to say, you need to buy even more tracking numbers as your Google organic search traffic grows. For high traffic websites, phone call tracking can get expensive very fast.

If you do not follow the daily visitors/40 tracking numbers rule, your likelihood score will fall over time and you will see data discrepancies between your call tracking and GA reports.

Pricing

In the case of CTM it costs around $2 to buy local phone numbers and around $4 for toll free numbers, plus you also need to pay around 5 cents per minute of call duration.

The actual rates depend upon the pricing plan you select and the country you operate in.

I would recommend that you buy tracking numbers for each of the following tracking sources:

1. Direct traffic.
2. Google organic.
3. Google paid.
4. Bing paid.
5. Referrals.
6. Email.

When you set up a new tracking number in your call tracking software, you need to specify the **receiving number** and the **tracking source**.

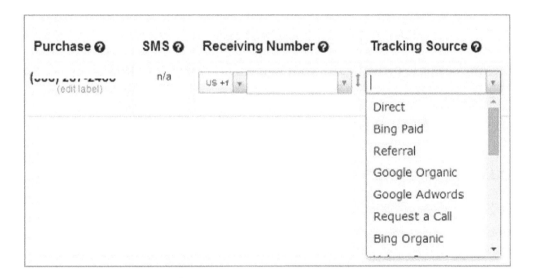

The receiving number is the phone number to which calls will be forwarded to, from the tracking number.

In case of TV, print, outdoor and radio ads, a person is assumed to make a call using the number displayed on the advertising channel.

For example, if a person saw your phone number (a unique tracking number for TV) on a TV ad, then he is assumed to make a call using that number.

As soon as he makes a call, the call tracking software sets the tracking source to 'TV ad' and starts recording more details about the caller and his conversation.

Needless to say, you would need to buy at least one unique tracking number each for TV, print, outdoor and radio campaigns.

"The more tracking numbers you buy, the more you can segment the data."

Just imagine, if you buy one unique tracking number for each display ad, you can then track the performance of each display ad individually.

3. Copy and paste the call tracking script

The call tracking script is provided by your call tracking vendor and needs to be placed on each and every page of your website. The script is generally placed in the head section (between the <HEAD> and </HEAD> tags).

4. Add call centre staff as users to your call tracking software

This is a very important step in phone call tracking as it allows you to calculate the ROI of your phone call tracking efforts.

Every call centre agent must use call tracking software all the time to tag calls (more about this later).

5. Link your call tracking account to your Google Analytics account

By doing this you can import call data into Google Analytics.

Step 3. Setting up phone calls as goal conversions in Google Analytics

Some call tracking software sends call data to GA via events while others send data via virtual pageviews.

If your call tracking software is sending call data via events (and it should be doing that), you can then see the phone call data in the 'top events' report (under 'behavior', then 'events' in your GA account).

Look for the event category called 'calls' to see the phone call data in GA:

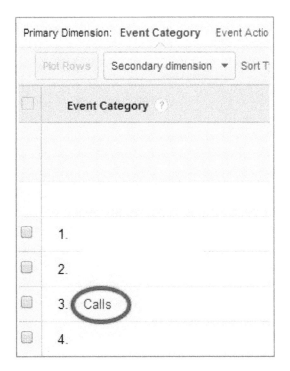

The call data is structured and reported in GA in the same way as event data:

GA Event Field	Call Tracking Data Value
Category	Calls
Action	Tracking Source like 'Google Organic', 'Google Adwords', 'Direct', 'Email' etc
Label	Caller Information like caller phone number, call type (first call or repeated call) & caller id
Value	Length of the phone calls in seconds

For example:

Event Category	Event Action	Event Label	Event Value
			57.010
			% of Total: 5 ...3)
			Z ≡ ≡ ⇄
1. Calls	1. Google Adwords	1. "not set", ...3:first-call, 6...	3 (0.52%)
2. CallSale	2. Google Organic	2. "not set", + ...3:first-call,	2 (0.61%)
	3. Bing Organic	3. "not set", + ...3:first-call, ...	3 (0.71%)
	4. Direct	4. "not set", + ...3:repeat-call,	1 2 (1.99%)
	5. Referral	5. "not set", + ...3:repeat-call,	2 (0.28%)
	6. Yahoo Organic	6. "not set", + ...3:repeat-call,	1 1 (1.88%)

Note: Event category, event action and event label are available as dimensions in GA reports whereas event value is available as a metric. For the sake of simplicity I have put all the values of event category, event action, event label and event value together side-by-side in the screenshot above.

You can see that there is one more event category called **'CallSale'** which stores phone call data. The CTM software use this special event category to import the number of phone calls which resulted in sales to GA. I will tell you more about this category later.

Now you know how the call data is structured in GA reports, you can use this information to set phone calls as event goals in GA.

For example, you can use the following configuration to track the total number of phone calls in GA:

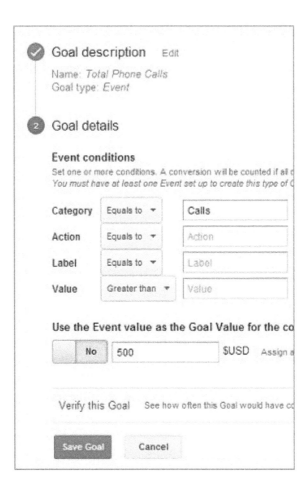

Note: When you leave the action field, label field and value field blank, the event goal tracks all the calls. Make sure that you do not specify event value as the goal value. In the screenshot above, a phone call is worth $500 for the business. That is why I have added $500 as the goal value.

You can determine what a phone call is worth to you by doing this simple calculation:

> *Phone call value*
> *= total revenue generated through phone calls in a month/ total number of phone calls in a month*

This will give you the average value of a phone call which you can then use as a goal value.

Similarly, you can use the following configuration to track phone calls from Google organic search which are unique (i.e. not repeated calls from a same caller) and which are more than sixty seconds in time duration:

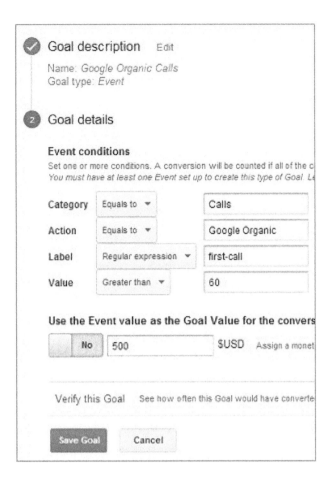

Note: The value of the 'label' field is 'first-call' which tells GA to track only when the caller calls for the first time and not to track repeated calls from the same caller.

Once you have set up phone calls as goals in GA, they will soon be available in all GA reports which have got the goals tab:

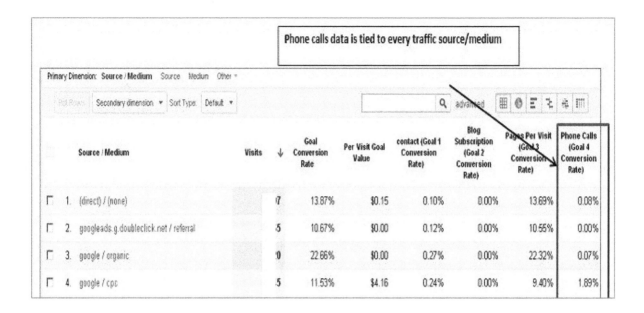

Step 4. Training call centre staff to make notes and score each phone call

This is the most important step of setting up phone call tracking. Yet not many talk about it.

> *"Your call tracking reports will be of little value if your call centre staff are not scoring each and every phone call."*

Scoring a phone call means giving it a star rating and assigning it a sales amount if it results in sales.

CTM uses a five star rating system which is used on the basis of how good or bad the phone call lead was.

For example:

1. If the phone call turned out to be a wrong number, then a CSR can give the call a one star rating. However, if you get a large volume of phone calls, you can choose not to score wrong numbers as scoring a call is time consuming.

2. If the caller seems very interested in making a purchase then the CSR can give the call a four star rating.

3. If the caller make a purchase then the CSR can give the call a five star rating and at the same time assign a monetary value to it. This monetary value is equal to the price for which a product/service was sold over the phone.

Scoring a call

Follow the steps below to score a phone call in CTM:

1. Go to the 'call log' report under the 'calls' menu:

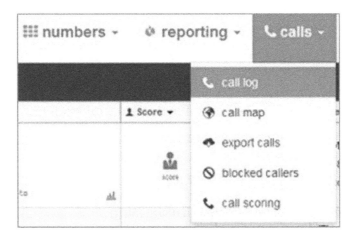

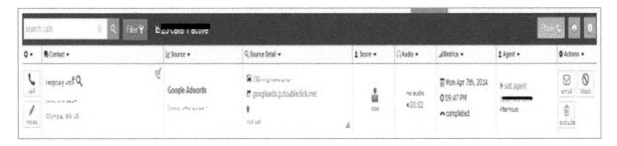

2. Click on the 'notes' button:

This button is used to make notes about each phone call. Once you click on this button, you will see a dialog box like the one below:

You need to train your call centre staff to make notes about each phone call (whether inbound or outbound) either during a call or after the call.

> *"Most CSR prefer to make notes during the call as making notes after a phone call can leave other callers in waiting."*

The **notes text field** is used to make notes by the CSR whereas the **tags text field** is used to **tag each phone call**.

You can enter any tag you wish. You can add tags like 'follow up', 'good lead', 'big party', 'new caller', 'repeat callers', 'hang up', 'inquiry' etc.

The tag field will prepopulate based on tags you have previously used. These tags can later help you in filtering call tracking data from reports.

Now click on the **'sale' tab.** You will see a dialog box like the one below:

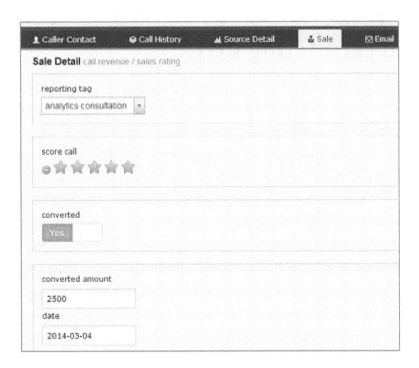

This dialog box is used to score each phone call. It is very important that you score each call by giving it a star rating. This will help you later in ROI reporting.

The **reporting tag** is another way to classify your calls (you can use product/service name, product code, etc.).

If the phone call resulted in a sale, then you must switch on the 'converted' button and enter converted amount and the conversion date.

For example, in the screenshot above, I rate the call five star because it resulted in a sale. Since the phone call resulted in a sale of £2,500, I entered 2,500 in the **converted amount text box** and specified the conversion date in the **date text box.**

The converted amount specified here automatically gets imported into Google Analytics reports via the special event category called **'CallSale'** as mentioned earlier. In this way you can determine the sales associated with a phone call.

Step 5. Entering your ad spend for each marketing channel and calculating ROI

> *"In order to calculate ROI of your phone call efforts, you need two metrics - sales and cost."*

You can calculate the sales figure by scoring each phone call as described earlier. The cost data is something which you will need to enter manually into your call tracking software every month for each marketing channel.

In the case of CTM, click on the 'ROI dashboard' under the 'reporting' menu. You will then see a form where you can enter your monthly ad spend for each marketing channel:

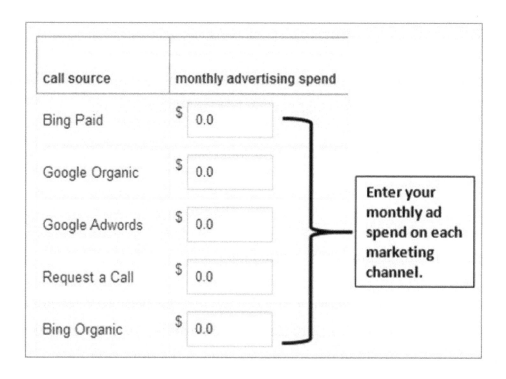

Note: you can and should exclude certain traffic sources from ROI reports (by clicking on the '**exclude source from ROI reports**' checkbox under the 'ROI settings' report), like direct traffic and referral traffic.

> *"Direct traffic is not a marketing channel but a behaviour which occurs as a result of investment in other marketing channels.*
>
> *Similarly, referral traffic is a by-product of investment in other marketing channels like SEO, PPC, email etc."*

Once you have supplied the cost data, your '**ROI dashboard**' will be automatically updated and you can see the ROI for each marketing channel:

New metrics to make your phone call tracking more effective.

call source	monthly advertising spend	calls	unique callers	cost / call	cost / caller	calls closed	% of calls closed	callers closed	% of callers closed	avg calls to close	total revenue	ROI
Google Paid	$ 450.0	541	403	$0.83	$1.11	4	0.0073%	4	0.0099%	1	$1050.0	133.33%
Youtube	$ 700.0	28	25	$25	$28	4	0.1428%	4	0.16%	1	$3393.0	384.71%
Bing Local	$ 700.0	17	16	$41.17	$43.75	2	0.1176%	2	0.125%	1	$1236.0	76.57%
Google Organic	$ 5000.0	5	4	$1000	$1250	3	0.6%	3	0.75%	1	$9704.0	94.08%

In this example:

Cost/call

> *Cost/call*
>
> *= monthly advertising spend on the call source / total calls from the same source.*

For example, in the case of Google paid search:

Cost/call

= $450/541

= $0.83

Cost/caller

> *Cost/caller*
>
> *= monthly advertising spend on the call source / total unique callers from the same source.*

For example, in the case of Google paid search:

Cost/caller

= $450/403

= $1.11

Calls closed

> *Calls closed*
>
> *= total number of call from a source which resulted in sales.*

For example in case of Google paid, the number of calls closed is four i.e. four calls resulted in sales from Google paid search in a month.

Percentage of calls closed

The percentage of phone calls which resulted in a sale. It is equal to calls closed/total calls.

Callers closed

The number of unique callers which made a purchase over the phone.

Percentage of callers closed

The percentage of unique callers which made a purchase over the phone. It is equal to callers closed/total unique callers.

Total revenue

The total revenue generated from a particular call source.

ROI

> *ROI*
>
> *= (total revenue from a call source – monthly advertising spend on the call source)/ monthly advertising spend on the call source.*

For example, in the case of Google paid search:

ROI
= ($1050 − $450) / $450
= 133.33 %

Step 6. Determining the performance of your call centre staff

The cool thing about using call tracking software is that you no longer need to guess the performance of your call centre staff and make faith-based decisions when it comes to performance appraisal.

Not only can you listen to the actual conversation between your CSR and a caller to determine how the CSR is handling calls but you can also go one step ahead and calculate revenue generated by each CSR.

To determine the CSR performance in CTM, go to '**reporting tags metrics'** report under 'ROI reports':

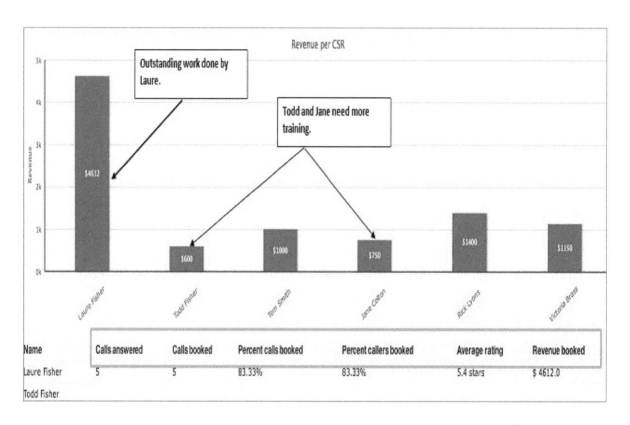

Name	Calls answered	Calls booked	Percent calls booked	Percent callers booked	Average rating	Revenue booked
Laure Fisher	5	5	83.33%	83.33%	5.4 stars	$ 4612.0
Todd Fisher						

Step 7. Creating custom reports for detailed phone call analysis in Google Analytics

Custom reports provide much more flexibility in terms of retrieving and reporting phone call data. I cannot tell you in advance what custom reports you should create as your situation and requirements are going to be different.

Below is one custom report which I find useful. You can create a custom report with the following specifications:

Metrics: total phone calls (goal completion), unique phone calls (goal completion), total phone calls (goal conversion rate), call sale (goal completion), call sale (goal conversion rate), sessions.

Dimensions drilldowns: default channel grouping, source/medium, landing page, keyword.

One big advantage of using custom reports is that you can easily retrieve **phone call goals volume** (in addition to phone call conversion rate) for each traffic source, which is not available in standard reports.

Lesson 6: Powerful methods to improve phone call conversion rate

If you look at the phone call conversion rate of your website, you will quickly find out that the majority of your site visitors do not choose to make a phone call. Although phone call conversion rates varies from industry to industry, I have yet to see a phone call conversion rate which is higher than 10%.

> *"The average phone call conversion rate is below 2%."*

That means 98% of the website visitors choose not to make a phone call. So what can be done to ensure more visitors make a call?

How you can increase your phone call conversion rate

1. Score each phone call

When you score each phone call, you can quickly determine which marketing channels are producing high quality phone call leads (which result in sales) and which are not. You can then choose to stop spending money on the channels which are constantly producing low quality phone leads.

2. Score each phone call!

Sometimes traffic is not the problem but your call centre staff are. You need to know how good your call centre staff are in converting phone leads into sales. If you are scoring each phone call, you can easily measure the performance of each CSR as explained earlier in this post.

3. Score each phone call!!

If you are scoring each phone call, you can easily calculate the ROI for each marketing channel. You can then choose to stop spending money on channels which are constantly producing negative ROI and spend more money on the channels which are constantly producing high ROI.

4. Collect caller names and phone numbers

If your business relies heavily on phone call leads then you should aim to collect as many caller names and phone numbers as possible through your website and marketing campaigns. For your business, collecting phone numbers is more important than collecting email addresses. In this way you can dramatically increase your phone call leads.

5. Make outbound phone calls

Many businesses rely heavily on inbound calls and make little to no efforts in collecting phone numbers and making outgoing calls. Do not just wait for people to call you. Be proactive and make calls.

6. Follow up within few minutes

You must follow up as soon as you get a phone lead. The longer you delay, the higher the probability that the lead will not turn into a sale.

7. Provide an outstanding phone call experience

You need to streamline the phone call experience you provide to the point that your callers are simply blown away by your service and recommend you to everyone. That means being super helpful and friendly and going out of your way to resolve callers' queries in a timely manner. Companies who do not do this end up wasting a lot of phone leads.

8. Set-up 'click to call' forms

Ordinary web-based forms do not work as well as 'click to call' forms when it comes to converting phone leads into sales. As soon as a person submits a 'click to call' form, your CSR receives a phone call asking him if he wants to take the call. Once he takes the call, the phone call is tracked alongside your other call reports. The biggest advantage of using 'click to call' forms is that you can follow up quickly, which is a very important factor in converting a phone lead into sales.

9. Follow landing page optimization best practices

If your main objective is getting a phone call, then this should be reflected in your landing page design. Place phone numbers prominently on your page with little to zero other CTAs (call to actions).

10. Conduct A/B testing

Place phone numbers in different locations on your landing page and A/B test them.

11. Listen to phone conversation between callers and your call centre staff

This can be a daunting task if you are getting hundreds of calls each day but sometimes this is the only way to improve phone call conversion rate when everything else has failed.

Every phone call you listen to is the equivalent of live customer feedback.

If you listen carefully and make notes along the way, you can hear customer objections. Once you have a list of common customer objections, then look for ways to remove such objections. This will improve your phone conversion rate.

Lesson 7: How to measure the ROI of content marketing

What makes content great? Is it uniqueness, informativeness, visual appeal, social shares, tons of backlinks or all of the above?

If you think that the greatness of content cannot be measured and the definition of great content is subjective then I strongly suggest that you reconsider your views, especially if the content you are developing is for commercial purposes.

> *"If content is not adding any value to your business's bottom-line then it is not great content."*

You may have a hard time justifying the cost of its production sooner or later, especially if you are spending crazy amounts of money on content development and marketing each month with no apparent return on investment in **monetary terms**.

Here is a commercial definition of great content:

> *"Great content is content (blog post, infographic, video etc.) which is most frequently viewed prior to conversion(s) and/or transaction(s) on your website."*

Here is the formula to calculate greatness:

Great content

= (total revenue which the content helped in generating + total value of the conversions which the content completed) / number of unique pageviews of the content prior to conversions and/or transactions.

I have not made up this formula. That is how Google Analytics calculates the economic value added by a piece of content to your business bottom-line in monetary terms.

In Google Analytics the metric which is used to calculate the greatness of a piece of content is known as page value (formerly known as **$index value**).

Let us understand page value through a case study.

Case study 1: What is my infographic worth?

Let us suppose that the production cost of your infographic was $400

Let us suppose the marketing cost of the infographic was $100 (time it took to promote the infographic * marketer's salary per hour)

So the total cost of the content production and marketing = $500

Now once you have published this infographic on your website, you need to **measure** what your site visitors did after viewing this infographic. I am not talking about measuring social sharing (number of tweets, Facebook likes etc.) or the number of back links the infographic acquired.

I am talking about determining the number of people who completed a conversion or made a purchase after viewing the infographic.

Let us suppose that your site visitors made a purchase worth $121 and completed conversions worth $50 after viewing the infographic. Let us also suppose that your infographic got 171 unique pageviews in total, prior to conversions and/or transactions.

Greatness of your infographic

= (total revenue + total goal value) / number of unique pageviews of the infographic prior to conversions and/or transactions

= ($121+ $50)/171

= $1

Google Analytics measure this greatness in terms of 'page value'.

Now head to the 'all pages' report (under 'behavior', then 'site content') in Google Analytics and sort the report by 'page value':

Page			Pageviews		Bounce Rate	% Exit	Page Value	↓
			% of					
1. /c			723 (0.75%)		20.00%	8.16%	A$71.92(1,113.90%)	
2. /t s	⦙-ca		1 (0.00%)		0.00%	0.00%	A$67.50(1,045.48%)	
3. /c			687 (0.71%)		9.09%	2.18%	A$67.04(1,038.29%)	
4. /c			564 (0.58%)		0.00%	3.90%	A$60.47(936.52%)	
5. /t n.	-48		5 (0.01%)		0.00%	0.00%	A$47.60(737.25%)	
6. /t	:s		11 (0.01%)		0.00%	9.09%	A$44.64(691.36%)	
7. /t			7 (0.01%)		100.00%	14.29%	A$43.07(667.11%)	
8. /t			21 (0.02%)		0.00%	4.76%	A$42.10(652.07%)	
9. /t			10 (0.01%)		100.00%	20.00%	A$35.00(542.10%)	
10. /t			15 (0.02%)		0.00%	6.67%	A$34.47(533.84%)	

From this report we can see that the maximum value added by a piece of content to the business bottom-line is $71.

Our infographic added a value of just $1.

Since page value is a ranking metric which is useful only when you compare it with the page values of other landing pages, our infographic has added very little value to the business bottom-line when you compare it with other piece of content on the website.

You need to do such type of comparisons when you are measuring greatness /profitability of a piece of content.

> *"The page value of $1 does not mean anything on its own. It is a ranking metric which means it is a metric which is useful only when you compare it with others."*

If you are still in doubt about the performance of the infographic (which I am sure you are), then check the performance of the landing page on which you published your infographic via the 'landing pages' report:

From the report above we can conclude that infographic resulted in sales of $121.

If you are a super geek, you will of course head to the 'assisted conversions' report (under 'conversions' then 'multi-channel funnels' in Google Analytics), to find out if the infographic played any role in assisting conversions, if not directly completing conversions.

To do this select 'landing page URL' as the primary dimension and then note down the assisted conversion volume and assisted conversion value of your infographic:

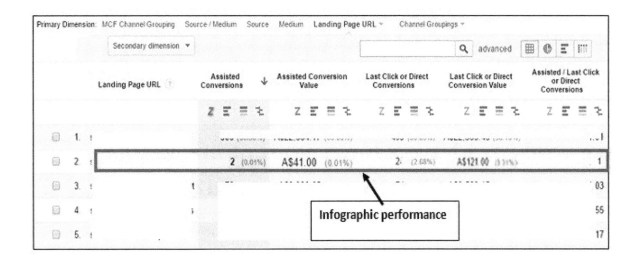

Here the assisted conversion value of our infographic is $41.

Total economic value added to the business bottom-line by our infographic
= total revenue which the infographic helped in generating (last click conversion value) +
total value of the conversions which infographic assisted (assisted conversion value)
= $121 + $41
= $162

Since the total economic value of $162 is less than the production and marketing cost of your infographic ($500), we can conclude that we have a negative return on our investment:

ROI

= (total economic value added by the infographic – production and marketing cost)/production and marketing cost

= ($162 – $500)/$500

= -67.6%

At this point you can show the links and social shares your infographic helped generate (which improved brand awareness and the SEO) and which may help in generating some indirect sales in the future.

However, you do not have any solid data to back up the claim that the infographic was worth the ROI.

Case study 2: I have a huge content marketing budget. How do I justify my ad spend?

Let's assume that your content marketing budget is $25,000 per month.

Reporting just social sharing and links is not going to help if the economic value added by the contents to the business bottom-line is very low or worse zero.

Reporting social shares and links is the equivalent of adding icing on a cake, provided you have the cake. Here the cake is your report, which shows the economic value added to the business bottom-line, and the icing is the secondary benefits such as links, social shares, brand visibility etc.

I called them secondary benefits because you cannot easily prove the impact of links, social shares, brand visibility etc. generated by your infographic on the business bottom-line in **monetary terms**.

If you present a cake without icing it may work. But if you present icing without cake then it not going to work.

If the contents you are producing are not adding any monetary value to the business bottom-line then you may, sooner or later, have a hard time justifying the cost of its production and marketing.

One quick way to determine which pages on your site are not adding any value to your business bottom-line is by looking at their page value. A page value of $0 means they have not added any value to your business bottom-line.

We often take content consumption and engagement (average time on page, pageviews, number of tweets, number of Facebook likes etc.) as a measure of success in content marketing.

But this content consumption and engagement may be for all the wrong reasons.

So before you declare content consumption or engagement as success, look at the page value metric. If it is a big $0 for every piece of content published on your website then your contents are not adding any monetary value to the business bottom-line, at least not in a manner which you can easily prove, and you should seriously reconsider your content strategies.

Some facts about the page value metric

1. Make sure that you have set up goals, goal values and enabled ecommerce reporting before you look at the page value metric. Otherwise you will see a page value of $0 for every piece of content.

2. Pages that were least frequently viewed prior to conversions or transactions get the lowest page value.

3. Pages that were not viewed prior to conversions or transactions get the zero page value.

4. Pages that were most frequently viewed prior to high value conversions or transactions get the highest page value.

5. Page value is not useful as a standalone metric. It is useful only as a point of comparison.

6. Do not measure the success of a piece of content on the basis of page value alone. You also need to look at the total economic value added by the content to the business bottom-line.

Social media hits do not always mean success

Your content marketing efforts cannot be considered a success just because they received a lot of tweets, pageviews, backlinks, Facebook likes etc.

Of course, social shares give that warm, fuzzy feeling but businesses do not run on warm, fuzzy feelings. So unless you write for personal delight, you need to compute the economic value added to the business by your content.

> *"Social media hits are not a guarantee of success."*

Your content must add value to the business bottom-line in monetary terms and you must be able to compute and show the monetary value added.

I have found that the following types of content can be social media hits but generally do not add any considerable economic value to the business bottom-line:

1. Curated contents.
2. Interviews.
3. Ego bait.

4. Infographics.
5. Content which criticize other individuals/businesses.
6. Content which has nothing to do with your target audience/market/products.

If your content marketing strategy is heavily focused on producing this type of content then I strongly suggest that you reconsider your strategy.

Of all the content I have analysed so far, I have found infographics to be the least profitable. The chances of their success is bleak, cost per acquisition is generally high and above all they can be very costly to produce.

The biggest mistake marketers make is producing content which has nothing to do with their target audience or niche.

> *"If you do not align your content marketing goals with your business goals then you cannot expect to improve your business bottom-line. It is as simple as that."*

Purge your analytics data before your measure content marketing

I have seen many analytics accounts where marketers set up and measure irrelevant goals and add random values to the goals they are measuring.

Such practices can greatly skew the conversion rate, page value, per session goal value, per session value and various other metrics across several analytics reports especially multi-channel funnel reports.

> *"Always question how the data is collected in the first place."*

It is wise that, before you measure your content marketing efforts, you make sure that you are measuring only those goals which are beneficial to your business.

Make sure that the true value is assigned to each goal. If you do not purge your analytics data then you will make incorrect business decisions which can result in the loss of revenue.

Lesson 8: Calculating true conversion rate

Whenever I get a new account, the first thing I do is dramatically improve the conversion rate of the website along with campaign performance, user engagement and content consumption.

You may say, "We all do that eventually".

But there is a difference. I do it a bit faster, say within a few minutes, and I do it without spending any time or money on fixing website usability and other conversion issues.

I am able to do that by abandoning 'Global Analytics'.

> *"Global Analytics is the analysis of a campaign/website on a global level."*

Following is the classical definition of goal conversion rate in Google Analytics:

> *Goal conversion rate*
> *= total goal completions \ visits from the whole world*

In Google Analytics the goal conversion rate is calculated as:

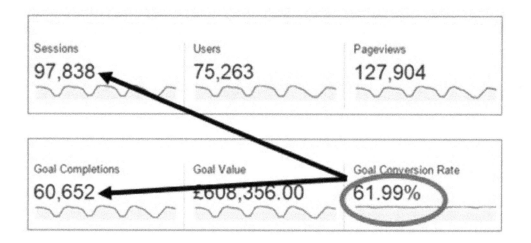

Note: Visits and sessions are the same thing in Google Analytics.

Goal conversion rate

= (goal completions / sessions)*100

= (60,652 / 97,838)*100

= 61.99%

Similarly, in Google Analytics the ecommerce conversion rate is calculated as:

Ecommerce conversion rate

= total transactions / visits from the whole world

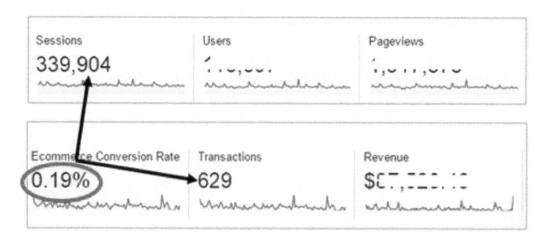

Ecommerce conversion rate

= (transactions/sessions) * 100

= (629/339,904 * 100

= 0.19%

Now a problem with such type of computation is that Google Analytics takes every person on the planet into account while calculating the conversion rate metric.

The website in question sells clothing only in the US and Canada but gets visits/sessions from around the world due to solid SEO and a huge social media presence.

Since people from other countries will not or cannot buy, you cannot hold them responsible for your sales.

But Google Analytics treats every person who has visited your website as a potential client and hence puts everyone in the conversion funnel while calculating the conversion rate metric.

There were more than 20,000 visits from the UK alone. These visits will never improve the bottom-line of my client's business as they are not the target market. So, what the people who generated these visits do on our website is irrelevant for tracking conversions, user engagement and content consumption.

They are simply not our target market. No matter what you do, you can never generate sales and leads through them. They should be filtered out from the conversion funnel along with all those people who came from other countries.

Look at this scenario the other way. If you sell car insurance in the UK you cannot say to your boss "we have low sales because people from Germany are not buying our insurance".

They will never buy your insurance because they are not your target market, however they can still visit your website through insurance related search terms or through social media.

When you pull the traditional conversion rate metrics from Google Analytics reports and present them to your client/boss, you are making people from non-UK countries responsible for your sales because the visits you have used for conversion rate calculations also include visits from non-UK countries and conversion rate is the percentage of **total website visits** which resulted in goals completion.

"As long as your conversion rate is the percentage of global visits which resulted in goals completion, you will never be able to determine the true conversion rate of your website."

So how you should calculate the true conversion rate?

> *Real goal conversion rate*
> *= total goal completions / visits from your target market*

> *Real ecommerce conversion rate*
> *= total transactions / visit from your target market*

Now let us calculate the real conversion rate of the website in question (the one which sells clothes in US and Canada).

Step 1: Create and apply a new advanced segment (named 'traffic from target market') in your Google Analytics view/profile which shows traffic only from your target market location. For example:

You can then see the true metrics for your website traffic:

You can now see how each and every metric in your Google Analytics report has changed dramatically. You are now looking at the real traffic data. The data which, until now, only a handful of super analytics ninjas were able to see.

All the metrics you see now are related only to your target market.

Check the new and true ecommerce conversion rate:

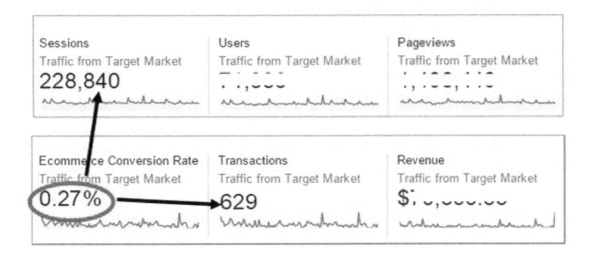

Your website ecommerce conversion rate now is 0.27%. Earlier it was 0.19%. Congratulations, you just improved your ecommerce conversion rate by 0.08 percentage points without fixing any conversion issues.

> *"Analytics is all about taking actions."*

Now what action can you take on the basis of this new and correct ecommerce conversion rate?

You need to look at the data and do something useful on the basis of the data you analysed with the aim to improve the business bottom-line.

Just knowing that the true ecommerce conversion rate is 0.27% will not improve your business bottom-line. You need to take action by following a process called **conversion optimization**.

Lesson 9: Analysing and reporting conversion rate

The goal conversion rate of a website is 61.99%:

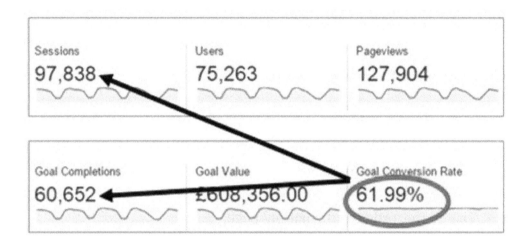

Ok good. But what insight you can get from it and what **action** can you take?

The short and sweet answer is **'nothing much'**.

> *"Google Analytics adds the conversion rate of each individual goal and then reports the sum as the overall conversion rate of the website. "*

So if you have set up five goals for your website in Google Analytics and the conversion rate of each goal turned out to be 20%, then Google Analytics will report **100% conversion** rate for your website.

So technically you have reached **marketing nirvana**. Go home, play video games or do whatever you like because your website cannot perform any better as it is able to convert all the website traffic into sales/leads.

But the reality is that your website can still perform much better. If you use Google Analytics, you can have a goal conversion rate greater than 100%, say 125%. You can even have a goal conversion rate of 500% and you can still be massively underperforming.

This is because in aggregate form you will never know which goal has contributed the most to your overall site conversion rate and whether the biggest contributor really has the biggest impact on your business bottom-line.

For example, consider the following scenario:

Goal 1: Visit to the 'newsletter' page.

Goal 2: Visit to the 'about us' page.

Goal 3: Visit to the 'order confirmation' page.

Goal 1 conversion rate: 40.49%.

Goal 2 conversion rate: 20.19%.

Goal 3 conversion rate: 1.31%.

In many industries, the goal which has the biggest impact on the bottom-line is the visit to the 'order confirmation' page (the page which is shown to a visitor when he/she completes a transaction).

The conversion rate of this goal is 1.31%. If you ignore this conversion rate and instead take the overall site conversion rate into account (which is 61.99%) then you will never know how your website is really performing.

> *"It is very important that you segment your overall goal conversion rate and look at the conversion rate of each goal."*

To see the conversion rate of each goal, login to your Google Analytics account, go to 'goals overview' report and then select the goal (whose conversion rate you want to analyse) from the 'all goals' drop down menu:

Goal Option:	
All Goals	
All Goals	174,336
Goal 4: Page	300
Goal 5: Page	467
Goal 6:	1,251
Goal 8: Consult	1,028
Goal 10:	650
Goal 11: minutes	170,240
Goal 13: Confirm	7
Goal 14:	188

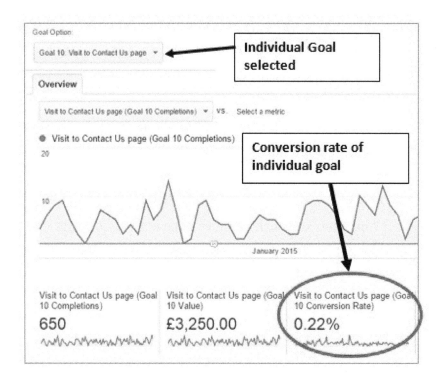

But even after all this segmentation, it is still a sub-optimal way of analysing conversion rates because you cannot take any action from such data. Therefore you need to segment this conversion rate further and analyse the conversion rate of each goal for each traffic source.

Go to 'all traffic', then 'source / medium report' in your Google Analytics account and then click on the 'goal set 1' tab.

You will see a report similar to the one below:

	Default Channel Grouping	Sessions		Goal Conversion Rate	Per Session Goal Value	Visit to Partner with us Page (Goal 4 Conversion Rate)	Visit to About Us Page (Goal 6 Conversion Rate)
			7	60.18% Avg for View: 60.18% (0.00%)	£6.09 Avg for View: £6.09 (0.00%)	0.10% Avg for View: 0.10% (0.00%)	0.43% Avg for View: 0.43% (0.00%)
	1. Organic Search	2		58.89%	£5.91	0.08%	0.33%
	2. Direct			65.53%	£7.18	0.16%	0.75%
	3. Email			74.36%	£7.50	0.18%	1.37%
	4. Social			67.72%	£6.90	0.39%	1.24%
	5. Referral			60.25%	£5.99	0.29%	0.91%
	6. (Other)			68.00%	£6.71	0.00%	1.09%
	7. Generic Paid Search			73.33%	£7.33	0.00%	0.00%

Focus on the conversion rate of each traffic source and conversion rate of each goal for each traffic source.

"Focus on the conversion rate of each traffic source and the conversion rate of each goal for each traffic source."

You now get a better picture of your website performance. The questions that you should be asking now are:

Question 1: What is the conversion rate of my goal named 'visit to partner with us page' for organic traffic and is there any improvement in this conversion rate in the last one month?

In other words you are determining how the traffic through organic search has impacted one of your website goal. If the goal conversion rate has gone down with the increase in organic traffic then maybe you are not targeting the right keywords?

Question 2: What is the conversion rate of my goal named 'visit to about us page' for email traffic and is there any improvement in this conversion rate in the last one month?

In other words you are determining how the traffic through email campaign has impacted your website goal. If goal conversion rate has gone down with the increase in email traffic then maybe you are not targeting the right people?

So instead of analysing and monitoring the overall conversion rate of the website, you are now analysing and monitoring the conversion rate of each goal for each traffic source.

Congratulations! You are now looking at the conversion rate data in a much better way than the majority of marketers out there. But unfortunately this is still a sub-optimal way of analysing the conversion rate, at least, it is for an analytics ninja.

> *"In order to truly analyse and report conversion rate, you need to focus on the conversion rate of each goal for each traffic source and for each target market."*

Many of us run marketing campaigns on national and international level. So it becomes very important for us to know how each main geographic location (it can be city, state or country) is performing in terms of improving the business bottom-line.

So the questions here to ask can be:

Question 3: What is the conversion rate of my goal named 'visit to partner with us page' for organic traffic in New York City and is there any improvement in this conversion rate in the last month?

This can be an important question to ask if your business serves people only from New York City.

Consequently you will not be interested in knowing what people from other parts of the country are doing on your website as they are not your target market.

In order to calculate the goal conversion rate of each goal for each traffic source in your target market (such as New York City), you need to create and apply an advanced segment (named 'traffic from New York City') which includes only the traffic from New York City.

Only then can you get a true picture of your website's performance:

"Focus on the conversion rate of each traffic source and the conversion rate of each goal for each traffic source in your target market"

If your target market is only New York City then you should be optimizing your campaigns on the basis of **New York City conversion rate** because this is all what that really matters for your business.

If you run marketing campaigns on an international level then you need to determine the conversion rate of each goal for each traffic source and in each top revenue generating country.

You can segment conversion rate further like segmenting conversion rate for new and returning users. There is virtually no limit to which you can segment the conversion rate metric.

The important point to remember here is, to segment the conversion rate metric and not take business and marketing decisions based on overall website conversion rate.

Lesson 10: Fundamental issues with the conversion rate metric

I have discovered the following issues with the conversion rate metric:

1. Data collection issues.
2. Data interpretation issues.
3. Statistical significance issues.
4. Data reporting issues.
5. Data optimization issues.
6. Unsuspected correlations between conversion rate and critical metrics.

Data collection issues with conversion rate

The manner in which web analytics tools, such as Google Analytics, collect conversion rate data is misleading and downright **wrong**. I talk about this in my earlier example.

Issue 1: Google Analytics add the goal conversion rate of each individual goal and then reports the sum as the overall goal conversion rate of the website. So if you have set up five goals for your website and the conversion rate of each goal turned out to be 20%, then Google Analytics will report 100% conversion rate for your website.

Issue 2: Google Analytics puts each and every visit to your site in the conversion funnel while computing goal conversion rates and ecommerce conversion rates. But this is never really the case. **Not every visit leads to conversion**. So the following traditional definitions of conversion rates are misleading and incorrect:

Goal conversion rate

= total goal completions/Total visits to the website

Ecommerce conversion rate

= total ecommerce transactions/total visits to the website

Issue 3: There are many ways of calculating conversion rate metric. You can calculate it by using total website sessions, website sessions only from the target market, unique sessions, users or unique users as denominator.

Consequently you can come up with different values of conversion rate for the same website goal.

Issue 4: When (i.e. period or event) the conversion rate was calculated can also have a big impact on its value. For example, the value of conversion rate varies when calculated in the peak season, off peak season, during aggressive sales campaigns, during major news about the business, during rapid decline or increase in website traffic.

Consequently you can have different values of conversion rate for the same website goal.

There are ways (data segmentation) to get around these issues but it is still a pain in the butt.

On the other hand conversion volume has no such data collection issues. You get what you see. If Google has reported 455 conversions through Google organic search than you have really got that many conversions through organic search.

Data interpretation issues with conversion rate

Since conversion rates calculated by analytics tools like Google Analytics do not represent the true conversion rate of a marketing channel, it is very easy to misinterpret them (unless you are a data segmentation junkie).

Another factor which contributes towards the misinterpretation of conversion rate data is its **ratio metrics** nature.

Ratio metrics are the metrics which are computed as ratio.

For example, bounce rate is a ratio metrics as it is computed as:

Bounce rate
= number of bounces/number of entrances

So what is the issue with ratio metrics?

Ratio metrics provide muddy analytical insight and can therefore horribly mislead you.

For example, consider the following scenario:

	E-Commerce Transactions	Total Visits	E-Commerce Conversion Rate
1st Month	5	1000	0.50%
2nd Month	50	10000	0.50%
3rd Month	210	41916	0.50%
4th Month	345	68848	0.50%
5th Month	392	78000	0.50%

According to the table above, your transaction volume has increased by more than 7,800% in the last five months, but since the focus is on ecommerce conversion rate there is virtually no improvement (flat 0.5% conversion rate as reported by Google Analytics, unless of course you bother to segment the data).

Consider another scenario:

	E-Commerce Transactions	Total Visits	E-Commerce Conversion Rate
6th Month	400	100,000	0.40%
7th Month	800	500,000	0.16%
8th Month	1000	800,000	0.13%

Here your transaction volume has increased by more than 19,900% in the last eight months, but since the focus is on ecommerce conversion rate there has been a sharp decline.

Since conversion volume is a **number metric**, you can never misinterpret it. 300 conversions mean 300 conversions. It is as simple as that.

Since conversion rate metric is horribly prone to misinterpretation, beware of the conversion optimization experts who boast of increasing the conversion rate of their client's website in double or triple digits like 280%.

Consider asking them the following questions:

Question 1: How has this 280% increase in conversion rate impacted the business bottom-line in monetary terms? Is the company which experienced such an uplift now a multi-billion dollar enterprise or are they still struggling to pay their utility bills?

Question 2: Is this a goal conversion rate or ecommerce conversion rate?

Question 3: Is this conversion rate in aggregated form or segmented?

Question 4: How was this conversion rate calculated? Using sessions? Unique visitors? By spending 280% more on marketing campaigns?

Question 5: When was this conversion rate calculated? Peak season? Off-peak season? During an aggressive sales campaign? During a rapid decline in traffic?

With so many questions to ask, it is hard to measure the performance of service providers who boast of their success in the form of conversion rate improvement.

"Always present conversion rate with context."

If I say to you that my website conversion rate is 15%, does it tell you anything meaningful about the site performance? No.

You do not know whether 15% is a good or bad conversion rate. You do not know whether the conversion rate has increased or decreased in comparison to last month. You do not know whether this conversion rate is a goal conversion rate or an ecommerce conversion rate.

You have no idea whether the reported conversion rate is in aggregated form or segmented.

In other words you are not aware of the context.

"Without context, data is meaningless. Comparison adds context to data and make it more meaningful."

So if you want to measure the performance of your marketing campaign, than you will need to compare its performance with last month's performance.

Without such comparison, you will never know whether or not you are making progress.

Consequently, the following report is not very useful:

	Conversion Rate	Orders
Jan	4.56%	2045

You can make this report more useful by comparing it with last month's performance.

	Conversion Rate	Orders
Jan	4.56%	2045
Dec	4.23%	1945

Statistical significance issues with conversion rate

The majority of us make marketing decisions on the basis of conversion rate. There is an industry trend to invest more in the marketing channel which has a higher conversion rate, but sometimes such thinking can backfire and it can backfire really badly.

> *"What if the marketing channel with a higher conversion rate is actually performing poorly and results in monetary loss if you invest in it?"*

Marketing decisions based on erroneous data cannot produce optimal results. So how accurate would your marketing decisions be if they are based on the erroneous conversion rate data?

You need to learn to fix this problem by determining whether your conversion rate is **statistically significant** (i.e. statistically meaningful).

For example, consider the performance of three campaigns A, B and C in the last month.

	E-Commerce Conversion Rate
Campaign A	8.25%
Campaign B	19.25%
Campaign C	5.24%

One look at this table and the majority of marketers will blindly assume that campaign B is performing much better than campaign A and campaign C because it has the highest conversion rate. So surely we should invest more in campaign B?

But wait a minute. Let us dig out how these conversion rates are actually calculated:

	Visits	Transactions	E-Commerce Conversion Rate
Campaign A	1820	150	8.25%
Campaign B	20	4	19.25%
Campaign C	780	41	5.24%

We can see from the chart above that the sample size in the case of campaign B is too small (four transactions out of 20 visits) to be statistically significant. Had campaign B got one transaction out of one visit, its conversion rate would be 100%. Will that make its performance even better? No.

So we can filter out campaign B performance while determining the best performing campaigns. I will explain in greater detail later why campaign B performance is statistically insignificant.

Now we are left with two campaigns, A and C. Clearly now campaign A is the winner because it has the higher conversion rate. But wait a minute. We are not done yet. We are still not sure whether the difference between the conversion rates of campaign A and Campaign C are statistically significant.

Let us assume that after conducting a statistical test we came to the conclusion that the difference in the conversion rates of the two campaigns cannot be proved to be statistically significant. Under these circumstances we cannot draw the conclusion that campaign C is not performing better.

So what can we do then? Well, we need to collect more data to compute statistical significance of the difference in the conversion rates of the two campaigns. At this stage investing more money in campaign A may not produce the optimal results that you may think it will.

Consider the following scenario:

From the table above we can see that the ecommerce conversion rate of Google CPC is higher than that of Google organic. Does that mean Google CPC campaigns are performing better than organic?

Before we jump to conclusions and invest more into PPC, let us calculate the statistical significance of the difference in conversion rates of Google organic and PPC campaigns by using a statistical test called a 'Z-test' in Google Analytics reports:

So according to my statistical test (Z-test), I have only 65% confidence that the difference in the conversion rates of Google organic and Google PPC is not by chance.

As confidence is less than 95%, the difference between the ecommerce conversion rate of Google organic and Google PPC is not statistically significant and we need to collect more data before drawing any conclusions.

There is one more very important thing that you need to remember here.

> *"It is possible and quite common for a result to be statistically significant and trivial or statistically insignificant but still important."*

For example, even if the difference in the conversion rates of Google organic and Google PPC turned out to be statistically significant we should still be investing more in Google organic (in this particular case) as the effect size (here revenue) of Google organic (which is $32k) is much larger than that of Google PPC (which is only $6k).

> *"In statistics 'effect' is the result of something. Effect size is the magnitude of the result."*

For example, if increasing the daily ad spend of a PPC campaign improves its conversion rate by 2% then 'improvement in conversion rate' is the 'effect' and 'improvement of 2%' is the 'effect size'.

> *"Just because a result is statistically significant, it does not always mean that it is practically meaningful."*

That is why we should interpret both the statistical significance and effect size of our results.

Data reporting issues with conversion rate

When you report conversion rates in aggregate form like 0.5%, your client has no idea what it means:

Is it 5 conversions out of 1,000 sessions or 50 conversions out of 10,000 sessions?

Are we making any progress and how can this progress be translated into monetary terms?

Since ratio metrics like conversion rate provides muddy analytical insight they **cannot effectively communicate your marketing efforts** to senior management/clients.

> *"Businesses understand numbers more than ratios."*

This is because numbers mean money and if you cannot **show them the money**; you will have a hard time getting anything done in SEO, PPC or any other form of marketing.

> *"Your client will be happier if you tell him that the number of orders on the website has doubled in the last three months than reporting something like; your website ecommerce conversion rate has improved by 0.431% in the last three months."*

Even if you report the conversion rate ratio, your client still needs to know the impact on the bottom-line, in the form of **number of orders.**

Conversion volume is a number and it communicates really well. Any person regardless of his background can easily understand that when his website received 300 orders in first month and 410 orders in second month, his online business is making progress.

Data optimization issues with conversion rate

It is **not very practical to optimize conversion rate** since it is a ratio metric.

You cannot set achievable targets for conversion rate such as improve the ecommerce conversion rate of the website by 1% in the next 6 months. This is because:

1. You cannot lead every visit and/or visitor to your website to convert, no matter what you do.

2. You will always get some/a lot of traffic which will not convert, no matter what you do.

3. Your website traffic will always increase (ideally it should) and it will not always increase in proportion to conversion volume.

4. Any person working in the marketing field long enough knows what a 1% increase in the conversion rate can do to your business bottom-line, especially at enterprise level. It can be the difference between making £1 million and £10 million.

Conversion volume on the other hand has no such data optimization issues.

> *"Since conversion volume is a number, you can easily set numerical targets for it."*

For example, "our target is to get at least 500 orders in the next six months" or "our target is to generate at least £50k a month in revenue in the next six months."

> *"Conversion volume is the total number of conversions or total monetary value of conversions in a given time period.*

A conversion can be a macro conversion like transactions, revenue, leads etc. and/or it can be a micro conversion like number of newsletter signups, file downloads etc."

In Google Analytics, conversion volume is called **goal completions**.

In Google Analytics standard reports, you will not see conversion volume in the way you would like to see it, for each traffic source. You need to create a custom report which lists conversion volume (a.k.a. goal completions) for each traffic source like the one below:

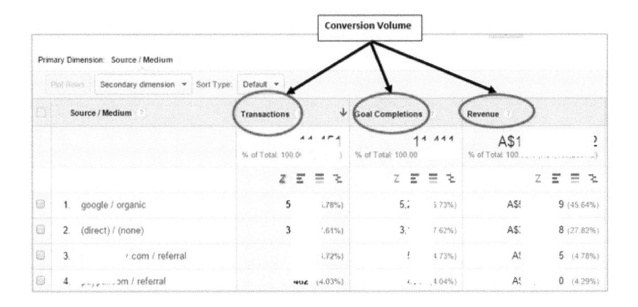

Lesson 11: Unsuspected correlations between conversion rate and critical business metrics

There is a common misconception among marketers that there is always a strong positive correlation between conversion rate and other business bottom-line impacting metrics such as revenue, orders, average order value and gross profit.

So as conversion rate increases there is always a corresponding increase in revenue, orders, average order value and gross profit.

Similarly, as conversion rate decreases there is always a corresponding decrease in revenue, orders, average order value and gross profit.

So improvement in conversion rate is a guarantee of improvement in business bottom-line.

However, this is not always the case as I will prove it to you in the next few minutes.

Negative correlation between conversion rate and average order value

When there is a negative correlation between conversion rate and average order value, as conversion rate increases there is a corresponding decrease in average order value and vice versa.

	Orders	Visits	Conversion Rate	Average Order Value	Product Revenue
March	300	7000	4.29%	150	45,000
April	400	8000	5.00%	100	40,000
% Change	33.33%	14.29%	16.67%	-33.33%	-11.11%

From the table above we can conclude that revenue declined by 11% even when the conversion rate improved by 16% in the last one month.

This happened because average order value declined by 33%. This proves that negative correlation can exist between conversion rate and average order value and increase in conversion rate does not always result in increase in sales.

Now look at the reverse scenario:

	Orders	Visits	Conversion Rate	Average Order Value	Product Revenue
March	400	8000	5.00%	100	40,000
April	300	7000	4.29%	150	45,000
% Change	-25.00%	-12.50%	-14.29%	50.00%	12.50%

From the table above we can conclude that revenue increased by 12% even when the conversion rate declined by 14% in the last month.

This happened because average order value increased by 50%. This again proves that negative correlation can exist between conversion rate and average order value and sales can increase despite of decline in conversion rate.

Negative correlation between conversion rate and orders

When there is a negative correlation between conversion rate and orders (also known as transactions), as conversion rate increases there is a corresponding decrease in number of orders and vice versa.

	Orders	Visits	Conversion Rate	Average Order Value	Product Revenue
March	400	8000	5.00%	100	40,000
April	300	5000	6.00%	100	30,000
% Change	-25.00%	-37.50%	20.00%	0.00%	-25.00%

From the table above we can conclude that revenue declined by 25% even when the conversion rate improved by 20% in the last one month.

This happened because number of orders declined by 25%. This proves that a negative correlation can exist between conversion rate and number of orders and an increase in conversion rate does not always result in an increase in revenue (i.e. sales).

Now let's look at the reverse scenario:

	Orders	Visits	Conversion Rate	Average Order Value	Product Revenue
March	300	5000	6.00%	100	30,000
April	400	8000	5.00%	100	40,000
% Change	33.33%	60.00%	-16.67%	0.00%	33.33%

From the table above we can conclude that revenue increased by 33% even when the conversion rate declined by 16% in the last month.

This happened because number of orders increased by 33%. This again proves that negative correlation can exist between conversion rate and number of orders and sales can increase despite a decline in conversion rate.

Negative correlation between conversion rate and gross profit

When there is a negative correlation between conversion rate and gross profit, as conversion rate increases there is a corresponding decrease in gross profit and vice versa.

	Orders	Visits	Conversion Rate	Average Order Value	Product Revenue	Acquisition Cost	Gross Profit
March	300	8000	3.75%	100	30,000	12000	18,000
April	310	4000	7.75%	100	31,000	15000	16,000
% Change	3.33%	-50.00%	106.67%	0.00%	3.33%	25.00%	-11.11%

From the table above we can conclude that gross profit declined by 11% even when the conversion rate improved by 106% in the last month.

This happened because acquisition cost (the cost of acquiring customers) increased by 25%. This proves that negative correlation can exist between conversion rate and gross profit and an increase in conversion rate does not always result in an increase in gross profit.

This situation generally occurs when we do not focus on cost per acquisition i.e. when we spend more time acquiring low value customers than the best customers.

Now look at the reverse scenario:

	Orders	Visits	Conversion Rate	Average Order Value	Product Revenue	Acquisition Cost	Gross Profit
March	300	4000	7.50%	100	30,000	15000	15,000
April	310	8000	3.88%	100	31,000	12000	19,000
% Change	3.33%	100.00%	-48.33%	0.00%	3.33%	-20.00%	26.67%

From the table above we can conclude that gross profit increased by 26% even when the conversion rate declined by 48% in the last month.

This happened because acquisition cost (the cost of acquiring customers) decreased by 20% and revenue increased by 3% in the last month. This proves that negative correlation can exist between conversion rate and gross profit and gross profit can increase despite a decline in conversion rate.

All of these case studies suggest that you should not be obsessed about improving the conversion rate metric and never make important business and marketing decisions just on the basis of this metric.

Lesson 12: Avoid making marketing decisions based on conversion rate

Somehow, in recent years, the conversion rate has become an even more important metric than ROI, especially for those internet marketers who sell **conversion rate optimization (CRO)** as a service to their clients.

Every second CRO agency boasts of improving the conversion rate of their clients by no less than two digits. Improving conversion rate by three digits is not uncommon either:

"80% improvement in conversion rate"
"300% improvement in conversion rate".

Sounds familiar?

Now the problem with these types of claims is that many of these agencies remain silent about the impact of increase in conversion rate on sales, cost and gross profit.

You will rarely see claims made like this one: "we improved the sales of our clients by 300%"

This is because:

> *"Increasing conversion rate is much easier than actually increasing the sales volume and gross profit."*

Example 1

Website A conversion volume = 100

Website A traffic = 10000 visits

Website A conversion rate

= 100/10000

= 1%

Now decrease the website traffic from 10k to 5k (pause some of the paid campaigns, they are not performing well).

Website A conversion rate

= 100/5000

= 2%

So now I can make the claim that I increased the conversion rate of website A by 100%. But does this improvement in conversion rate impact the business bottom-line? Does it improve sales? The answer is no!

Example 2

Website A conversion rate: 1%

Website A cost per acquisition: £20

After conversion rate improvement

Website A conversion rate: 2%

Website A cost per acquisition: £30

You may argue that an increase in conversion rate should decrease the acquisition cost. Well this is not always the case. In fact there is no direct correlation between conversion rate and cost. Your acquisition cost can easily go up if you are getting more average/low value customers than your best customers.

Remember:

> *Conversion rate*
> *= conversion volume/traffic.*

The calculation does not take cost into account. So any increase or decrease in cost will not directly impact the conversion rate. That also means any increase or decrease in conversion rate will not directly impact cost.

Example 3

Website A conversion rate: 1%

Website A sales: £200k

After conversion rate improvement:

Website A conversion rate: 2%

Website A sales: £150k

You may argue that an increase in conversion rate should increase the sales. Well this is not always the case. In fact there is a weak positive correlation between conversion rate and sales as conversion rate does not take **average order value** into account, an important part of increasing sales.

Remember:

> *Conversion rate*
> *= conversion volumes/traffic.*

The calculation does not take average order value into account. So any increase or decrease in average order value will not directly impact the conversion rate. That also means any increase or decrease in conversion rate will not directly impact average order value.

Your sales can go down even after an improvement in conversion rate, if there is a negative correlation between conversion rate and average order value or negative correlation between conversion rate and transactions as explained previously.

When someone is just promoting the importance of an increase in conversion rate, we have no idea:

1. How the improvement in conversion rate actually impacted the business bottom-line.
2. How the conversion rate metric was calculated.
3. Whether the conversion rate being reported is a goal conversion rate or an ecommerce conversion rate?
4. Whether the reported conversion rate is in aggregate form or segmented?
5. When the conversion rate metric was calculated?

How the improvement in conversion rate actually impacted the business bottom-line

Maybe there was only a marginal improvement in sales. May be there is no improvement in sales or may be the sales actually declined.

How the conversion rate metric was calculated

- Was conversion rate increased by increasing the conversion rate of the conversions which do not really impact the business bottom-line?
- Was conversion rate increased by decreasing the traffic?

- Was conversion rate increased by taking visitors into account instead of visits?
- Was conversion rate increased through some sneaky data segmentation?
- Was increase in conversion rate is a result of small data sample being used in testing?

Whether the conversion rate being promoted is a goal conversion rate or an ecommerce conversion rate

It is one thing to improve goal conversion rate by 5% but a totally difficult ball game, and much more difficult, to improve ecommerce conversion rate by 5%.

Whether the reported conversion rate is in aggregate form or segmented

If you have set up 5 goals and the conversion rate of each goal is 20%, then you would have a 100% website conversion rate. But does that mean your website is now converting every visitor into a customer? No.

When the conversion rate metric was calculated?

If it was calculated during peak season, then you are bound to have a high conversion rate.

So you see there are so many factors that you need to take into account while playing with the conversion rate metric. You cannot just blindly rely on conversion rate to improve the business bottom-line.

The solution is to monitor conversion volume and especially acquisition cost during conversion optimization.

There should be a considerable increase in conversion volume and a considerable decrease in acquisition cost if conversion optimization has actually been carried out.

Do not get blinded by a double/triple digit increase in conversion rate. It does not mean anything if there is little to no increase in conversion volume and gross profit.

Lesson 13: Why conversion volume is a better metric than conversion rate

Conversion rate calculations are horribly prone to errors

Conversion rate calculations are prone to different types of errors, including:

1. Observational errors
2. Computation errors
3. Statistical errors
4. Interpretation errors
5. Reporting errors

There will always be some sort of inaccuracy in conversion rate - no matter how much you segment the data – because it is a ratio metric. This is clearly not the case with conversion volume as it is a number metric.

Marketing decisions based on erroneous data cannot produce optimal results

Are you wondering how accurate your marketing decisions can be if they are based on the erroneous conversion rate data? Consider the following scenario:

	Visits	Transactions	E-Commerce Conversion Rate
Campaign A	1820	150	8.25%
Campaign B	20	4	19.25%
Campaign C	780	41	5.24%

Do you think you should be investing more in campaign B because its conversion rate is highest?

I would suggest not. The sample size in the case of campaign B (four transactions out of 20 visits) is too small to be statistically significant.

Do you think you should now be investing in campaign A because it has a higher conversion rate? Are you really sure that campaign A has a higher conversion rate than campaign B?

If the difference between the conversion rates of campaign A and campaign C is not statistically significant then campaign A does not have higher conversion rate.

Let us assume that after conducting a statistical test we came to the conclusion that the difference in the conversion rates of the two campaigns cannot be proved to be statistically significant.

Under these circumstances we cannot draw the conclusion that campaign C is not performing better. So what can we do? Well we need to collect more data to compute the statistical significance of the difference in the conversion rates of the two campaigns.

At this stage investing more money in campaign A may not produce optimal results as you may think it will.

Now let me ask you one more question:

How many times do you conduct a statistical test (like Z-test) to calculate the **confidence** that the difference in the conversion rates of the two or more campaigns is statistically significant before you declare one campaign as the winner and decide to invest more?[2]

Confidence
= (signal / noise) * √sample size

$$\text{confidence} = \frac{\text{signal}}{\text{noise}} \times \sqrt{\text{sample size.}}$$

I can bet that only a handful of marketers/analysts go through this hassle. Can you see yourself conducting such statistical tests, day in, day out, every time you look at your conversion rate reports?

Conversion volumes reflect **effect size** (signal) much more accurately than conversion rate.

This is one of the biggest reasons to use conversion volumes while taking marketing decisions.

> *"It is possible and quite common for a result to be statistically significant and trivial or statistically insignificant but still important."*

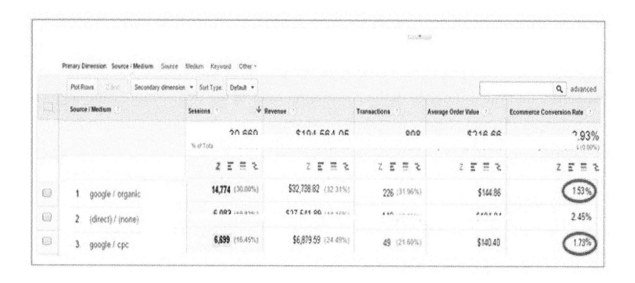

From the table above we can conclude that the ecommerce conversion rate of Google CPC is higher than that of Google Organic. Does that mean Google CPC campaigns are performing better than organic campaigns?

Before we jump to any conclusions and invest more in PPC, let us calculate the statistical significance of the difference in conversion rates of Google organic and PPC campaigns.

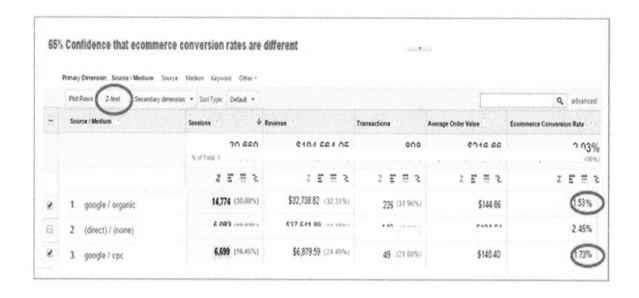

According to my statistical test (Z-test), I have only 65% confidence that the difference in the conversion rates of Google organic and Google PPC is not by chance.

"As confidence is less than 95% the difference is not statistically significant and we need to collect more data before drawing any conclusions."

Even if the difference in the conversion rates of Google organic and Google PPC turned out to be statistically significant we should still be investing more in Google organic (in this particular case) as the effect size (here revenue) of Google organic is much larger than that of Google PPC.

"Just because a result is statistically significant, it does not always mean that it is practically meaningful."

That is why we should interpret both the statistical significance and effect size of our results. This makes conversion volume such a powerful metric.

Conversions volume goes well with regular people. You do not need to be a geek to understand conversion volume. Conversion volume reflects marketing efforts much better than conversion rate and is easy to communicate with people from all walks of life.

Nobody cares what your conversion rate is, if the sales are going down. Your site conversion rate may be increasing but sales may still be going down. This is possible if traffic to your website is declining.

Conversion volume can be optimized

You can use conversion volume in any analytics framework that you create for your business. This is because you can set **achievable targets** for them.

You cannot set achievable numerical targets for conversion rates with any ease.

Conversion volume is error free

Conversion volume is not prone to errors (observational errors, computation errors, statistical errors, interpretation errors, reporting errors etc.) and is independent of conversion rate and other factors, such as website traffic.

So whenever there is a trade-off between conversion volume and conversion rate, support conversion volume any time of the day.

So the smart questions to ask now are:

Question 1. How many orders did I get through Google organic search in the last month and how much has conversion volume (not conversion rate) improved?

Question 2. How many leads did I get through email campaigns in the last month and how much has conversion volume (not conversion rate) improved?

Question 3. How many orders should we aim for in the next six months?

In the end, conversion volume is what matters the most to a business because it speaks the universal language (the language of money) loud and clear.

Lesson 14: Why you should stop optimizing for conversion rate

One might find it odd to talk about not doing conversion rate optimization (CRO) when CRO is one of the most popular ways of increasing conversions for a web based business. But, as odd as it may sound:

> *"CRO has always been the sub optimal way of optimizing your business performance."*

Many analysts are familiar with the limitations of CRO and never really say or do CRO. But by and large CRO is still considered as the most effective way to increase she ales/revenue of a website.

What is the problem with CRO?

CRO is just another form of obsession with a single metric (the conversion rate). When we are too obsessed with any one metric we tend to lose focus on bigger picture i.e. the business bottom-line, the net profit.

In the next few minutes I will convince you why CRO is a sub-optimal way of optimizing your business bottom-line and why you should focus on optimizing business metrics like revenue and cost.

Conversion rate is not that powerful

Contrary to popular belief, conversion rate has a weak positive correlation with revenue and zero correlation with cost.

> *"The two metrics that actually drive revenue are 'average order value' and 'number of transactions'."*

Conversion rate on the other hand has a secondary impact on revenue because it does not take into account 'average order value' in its calculation and it is a ratio metric in which the increase in traffic (visits) always tends to lower the value of the conversion rate.

You know by now that it is quite possible and common that:

1. An increase in conversion rate can result in a decrease in revenue.
2. A decrease in conversion rate can result in an increase in revenue.
3. An increase in conversion rate can actually result in a decrease in gross profit.

Because of the secondary impact of conversion rate on revenue and zero impact on the cost, it is no more important than a metric such as bounce rate... OK, I admit, it is a little bit more important than bounce rate.

But just as you would not measure the success or failure of your marketing efforts only on the basis of bounce rate, you also would not measure the success or failure of your marketing efforts only on the basis of conversion rate.

> *"In order to truly optimize revenue you need to focus on increasing average order value and the number of transactions for each of your market segment, product categories and other portfolios of outcomes."*

So next time you carry out a test to optimize your business performance, focus on how the change is impacting the average order value, transactions volume and the acquisition cost. Do not be fooled by the misleading conversion rate metric.

"When you say that you do CRO, you imply that all of your marketing efforts are conversion rate centric. You imply that all you care about is increasing conversion rate."

In order to get the optimum results from your marketing efforts, you need to focus on the metrics that really matters i.e. revenue and cost.

Therefore, when you change your focus from conversion rate to more useful metrics like revenue and cost, you are no longer doing CRO as your marketing efforts are no longer conversion rate centric.

You cannot really optimize conversion rate

As odd as it may sound, and despite the millions of blog posts and books out there teaching you CRO, you cannot really optimize conversion rate.

Following are two simple reasons:

1. Web analytics tools such as Google Analytics puts each and every visit to your website in the conversion funnel while computing conversion rates.

Not every visit leads to conversion, yet the formula for calculating the conversion rate is:

Conversion rate
= number of transactions/total visits

The question that arises is; can you really optimize each and every visit on your website for conversion? And the answer is 'no, you cannot'. You will always get some traffic which will not convert.

2. Let us assume that you calculate conversion rate differently. Instead of taking visits into account, you take visitors into account.

So your formula for calculating the conversion rate is now:

> *Conversion rate*
> *= number of transactions/total visitors.*

Now, the question that arises is; can you really optimize each and every visitor of your website for conversion? And the answer is 'no, you cannot'. You will always get some visitors which will not convert.

These visitors could be job seekers, competitors, link builders or on your website for any number of reasons other than completing a goal conversion or placing an order.

Other than these two simple reasons the conversion rate metric is innately prone to errors simply because it is a ratio metric. The ever increasing traffic on your website will always tend to lower the conversion rate.

Since conversion rate is a ratio metric, you cannot set achievable targets for it with any ease, for example, increasing the conversion rate by 5% in the next six months.

> *"Conversion rates are horribly prone to misinterpretation."*

In the case of conversion rate you do not always get what you see.

> *"Conversion rate has statistical significance issues, data collection, data interpretation and data reporting issues."*

What is conversion rate good for?

So, should you abandon the conversion rate metric completely?

No, I am not saying to discard the conversion rate metric.

"Conversion rate is a good indicator of quality of traffic to your website and also an effective way to determine website issues".

If you really want to use this metric then use, report and analyse conversion rates in segmented form and alongside conversion volume, not as a standalone metric.

If you are not segmenting the data the way it should be segmented, if you are not taking conversion volumes, statistical significance and confidence into account, then your conversion rate focus strategy will not produce optimal results and you may even incur huge losses.

Lesson 15: Understanding averages

Any set of measurements has two important properties:

1. The central value.
2. The spread about that value.

We calculate the central value with the aim to determine a typical value in a data set.

> *"A data set is a set of observed values for a particular variable, for example, average time on website."*

We measure the spread with the aim to determine how similar or varied the set of observed values in a data set are.

If the set of observed values are similar then the average (or mean) can be a good representative of all the values in the data set.

If the set of observed values vary by a large degree than the average (or mean) is not a good representative of all the values in the data set.

> *"We calculate the central value through mean, median and mode.*
>
> *We measure the spread of data values through range, interquartile range (IQR), variance and standard deviation."*

Understanding arithmetic mean

The mean (also known as arithmetic mean or population mean) is simply an average of the numbers. It is denoted by Greek letter μ ("mu").

The mean is calculated as:

Mean

= sum of numbers/count of numbers

For example, let us imagine a website has five web pages:

	Bounce Rate
Page 1	35%
Page 2	40%
Page 3	0%
Page 4	48%
Page 5	100%

Bounce rate of the site

= (35 + 40 + 0 + 48 + 100) / 5

= 223 / 5

= 44.6%

But is 44.6% a true bounce rate? No.

Look at the distribution of bounce rate across all the web pages. Page three and page five have extreme values of 0% and 100%. We call such values **outliers** in statistics.

Outliers have the sadistic ability to skew averages.

Similarly:

	Average time on page (in seconds)
Page 1	350
Page 2	400
Page 3	500
Page 4	480
Page 5	36000

Average time on the site

= (350 + 400 + 500 + 480 + 36000) / 5

= 37730 / 5

= 7546 seconds

= 2 hrs 6 minutes

But is 2 hours 6 minutes a true representation of the average time on a page? No.

Look at the distribution of average time across all the web pages. Page five has an extreme value of 36,000. Again the outlier 36,000 is skewing our average metric.

This is the fundamental problem with averages. The tragedy is that Google Analytics use this metric throughout its reports: average time on page, average time on site, site average... You cannot really escape from averages.

As long you keep analysing and reporting these average metrics you will get average results.

Understanding median

Median is the middle number in a sorted list of numbers.

For example, let us imagine a website has got five web pages:

	Bounce Rate
Page 1	35%
Page 2	40%
Page 3	0%
Page 4	48%
Page 5	100%

Let us first sort the list: 0%, 35%, 40%, 48%, 100%.

If we calculate the median (instead of mean) of this data set then it will be 40%.

Now is 40% a true representative of a typical bounce rate of the site? Yes.

This is because unlike mean, the median (or middle value) is not impacted by outliers (in our case: 0% and 100%).

Similarly:

	Average time on page (in seconds)
Page 1	350
Page 2	400
Page 3	500
Page 4	480
Page 5	36000

Let us first sort the list:

350, 400, 480, 500, 36000.

The middle number is 480.

The median of the data set is 480.

Now is 480 seconds (8 minutes) a true representative of a typical time spent on a web page? Yes.

This is because unlike mean, the median (or middle value) is not impacted by outliers (in our case 36,000).

You can always download analytics data/report into Excel and calculate the median of any data set (no matter how large) through the MEDIAN Excel function.

So, should you calculate the median all day long?

Calculating the median of each and every data set can be very time consuming and not practical for many.

What is the solution?

The solution is to first measure the spread of the data values in a data set and then decide whether or not you can trust the average value reported by your analytics tool, such as Google Analytics.

Measuring spread

There are two ways of measuring the spread:

1. Look at the distribution of values in a data set and find and eliminate outliers (or extreme values)

I use this method the majority of the time.

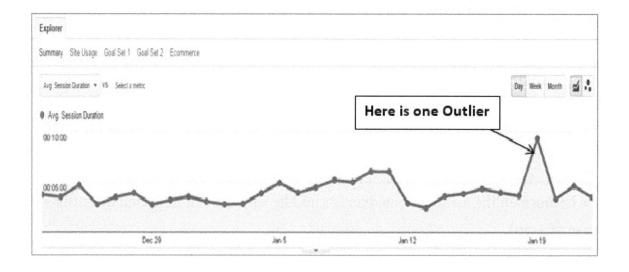

We measure the spread by calculating the **range**. The range is simply the difference between the maximum value and the minimum value in a data set.

> *Range*
> = maximum *value – minimum value*

If you look at the chart above, the minimum value is approximately 4 minutes and 30 seconds and the maximum value is approximately 9 minutes and 30 seconds.

Range

= 9 minutes 30 seconds – 4 minutes 30 seconds

= 5 minutes

If you look at the chart again, there is one outlier (or extreme value) of approximately 9 minutes and 30 seconds.

This outlier is skewing the **average session duration** because it has increased the value of the range. If we discount this outlier than the new maximum value would be approximately 5 minutes 30 seconds. So now the range is:

Range

= 5 minutes 30 seconds – 4 minutes 30 seconds

= 1 minute

> *"A small range indicates that the central value (in our case the average session duration) is a better representative of the typical value in a data set."*

If we discount the outlier and then calculate the average visit duration then we will get a better central value or typical value.

That is why it is important that we look at the distribution of values, calculate the spread and identify and discount outliers before we choose to trust an average metric/value.

Granted, this is not the most accurate way to measure spread and determine the central value but it is practical and it works; especially when you have to look at hundreds of reports per day and you do not have time to calculate median or spread through interquartile range (IQR).

So, instead of blindly relying on averages look at the distribution of data points. Determine how narrow or widespread the distribution of values in a data set is by calculating the range.

A very widespread distribution means you cannot rely on the average metric.

Average metrics do not just haunt Google Analytics reports; you can also find them haunting Google Webmaster Tools reports.

Do not rely on the average position:

Query	Impressions ▲	Clicks	CTR	Avg. position
	3,500	600	17%	4.1
	3,000	1,300	43%	1.0

This average position is a lie. Don't you get fooled by it.

Download this table   Show 25 rows ▼   1-25 of 3,201 ‹ ›

Look at the distribution of ranking positions instead:

Position in search results	Impressions ▲	Clicks
2	900	170
6 to 10	820	109
3	700	110
1	500	150
4	250	35
5	250	35
2nd page	57	35
3rd page +	15	10

If you are ranking from position 2 to '3rd page +' (or you could say position 2 to position 30+) for a search query then you cannot rely on an average value. This is because the range of ranking positions is too large.

You do not need to manually calculate the range here. It is quite evident from the distribution. That is why I urge to look at the distribution.

> *"If you do not measure the spread of data values you will never know whether or not your average value is a true representative of the typical value in a data set.*
>
> *That is why it is important that you calculate both the central value and the spread of the data values. "*

Note: You can calculate the range in Excel by using the formulas MAX and MIN.

For example:

=MAX(F4:P4)-MIN(F4:P4)

Here F4:P4 is a cell range.

MAX returns the largest value and MIN returns the lowest value in a set of values.

2. Through interquartile range (IQR), variance or standard deviation

This is the more difficult and time consuming way of calculating spread.

If you have a very large data set with a lot of outliers then you cannot depend upon the visual method I explained above to determine the spread of data values. In this case you would use IQR, variance or standard deviation to calculate the spread.

I recommend using IQR. It is a better measure of spread than the range or standard deviation because it is less likely to be distorted by outliers. So you calculate the IQR and then decide whether you can rely on the average value reported by your analytics tools.

Understanding interquartile range (IQR)

In order to understand IQR, you first need to understand quartiles.

> *A quartile is one of the four equal groups in which a data set can be divided.*

For example, consider the following ordered data set:

| 4 | 6 | 10 | 14 | 15 | 16 | 17 | 17 | 18 | 20 | 20 |

Here the point between the lowest 25% of the values is called the **25th percentile or the lower quartile**. The lower quartile is denoted by Q1.

The point between the 50% of the values is called the 50th percentile or the second quartile. This second quartile is actually the median. So the median is also denoted by Q2.

The point between the lowest 75% of the values is called the **75th percentile or the upper quartile**. The upper quartile is denoted by Q3.

> *"The difference between the upper quartile and lower quartile is called the interquartile range."*

> *Interquartile range = Q3-Q1*

In Excel 2010 there is a function called QUARTILE which allows you to calculate Q1, Q3 and eventually IQR.

The syntax to use this function is:

> *=QUARTILE (array, quart)*

Array is the range of cells which contains the data set.

Quart is the parameter which is used to specify which quartile to return. It can have three values: first quartile, median value and third quartile as shown below:

	TRANSPOSE		▾	✕ ✓ *fx*	=QUARTILE.EXC(B4:L4,						
	A	B	C	D	QUARTILE.EXC(array, **quart**)			I	J	K	L
1								1 - First quartile (25th percentile)			
2								2 - Median value (50th percentile)			
3								3 - Third quartile (75th percentile)			
4			4	6	10	14	15	16	17	17	18	20	20
5											
6											
7		Q1	4:L4,								

Through the QUARTILE function you can calculate the first and third quartile.

Once you have done this then find IQR using the formula Q3-Q1:

	C9			f_x	=C8-C7							
	A	B	C	D	E	F	G	H	I	J	K	L
1												
2												
3												
4		4	6	10	14	15	16	17	17	18	20	20
5												
6		Range	16									
7		Q1	10									
8		Q3	18									
9		IQR	8									

The data values that deviate from the middle value by more than twice the IQR are **outliers**.

The data values that deviate from the middle value by more than 3.5 times the IQR are called **far outliers**.

How the average metric is abused

Nobody wants to be average and yet we all love averages. That is why our analytics and research reports are all jam packed with averages.

> *"In order to analyse and report above average we first need to stop being obsessed with all the metrics which are 'average' and take the insight they provide with a huge grain of salt."*

Let us suppose that someone conducted a study of 1,500 posts from five different Facebook fan pages over three months and came up with the following results:

	Advertising Value of Posts
Fan Page A	£245.00
Fan Page B	£34.00
Fan Page C	£47.00
Fan Page D	£87.00
Fan Page E	£34.00
Mean	£89.40
Median	£47.00
Mode	£34.00

If you use **mean** as the average then it looks like the Facebook posts are worth a lot.

If you use **mode** as the average then it looks like the Facebook posts are not worth that much.

So, if you are selling advertising, which type of average is more profitable for you to report? Obviously the answer is mean.

Now let us suppose someone conducted a second study of 1,500 posts from five different Facebook fan pages over three months and came up with the following results:

	Advertising Value of Posts
Fan Page A	£45.00
Fan Page B	£35.00
Fan Page C	£30.00
Fan Page D	£0.00
Fan Page E	£0.00
Mean	£22.00
Median	£30.00
Mode	£0.00

Here the median is more than the mean, so why not use median here to increase the advertising value of posts.

This is just one example. You will often read studies and reports where a researcher will give you no explanation of the **choice of average** being used.

Ask yourself, is he using the average which helps him in reaching his conclusion? Maybe.

> *"It is very human to twist the data (either knowingly or unknowingly) to reach the conclusion one wants."*

So, what is the solution?

First measure the spread of the data values in a data set and then decide whether or not you can trust the reported average value.

You can measure the spread either by looking at the distribution of values in a data set or by calculating spread through IQR, variance or standard deviation.

Another powerful method to reduce the negative impact of average metrics on your analysis and business decisions is **data segmentation**.

> *"The more you segment the data, the smaller the data set and the data values will be and the closer to the mean or average value."*

In other words, the more you segment the data, the more accurate your average metrics will be.

For this reason, you will get a better insight if you analyse the goal conversion rate of organic search for each of your goals in your target market (e.g. New York), rather than analysing the conversion rate of the organic search for all of the locations from which your website receives traffic.

Lesson 16: Important business metrics

Percentage change (percentage of rise or fall)

This metric is used to calculate the percentage of rise or fall in relation to the old value. We use percentage change when there is an old value and a new value.

Percentage change
= ((new value – old value) / old value) * 100

For example:

	Visits	Conversions	Conversion Rate
July	200	20	10%
Aug	350	42	12%
% Change	75%	110%	20%

Visits percentage change
= ((350 - 200) / 200) * 100
= 75%

Conversions percentage change

= ((42 - 20) / 20) * 100

= 110%

Conversion rate percentage change

= ((12 - 10) / 10) * 100

= 20%

Google Analytics calculates the percentage change (for every type of metric) when you compare the data with the past data.

Imagine if pages per session in July were 2 and in August there were 4. You should not report that pages per session has improved by 2. You report that pages/session has improved by 100% (the percentage of change from the old value).

Similarly, we can calculate the percentage change for average visit duration, percentage of new sessions, bounce rate etc.

Percentage difference (percentage difference between two values)

The percentage difference metric is used to calculate the difference between two values in a percentage. Use this metric when neither value is more important than the other.

> *Percentage difference*
> *= (| difference between two values | / average of the two values) * 100*

Please note: The use of vertical bars on each side of a value denote an **absolute value** (or modulus).

For example:

	Visits	Conversion Rate
July	200	10%
Aug	350	12%
% Change	75%	20%
% Difference	54.54%	18.18%

Percentage difference

= (| 200 − 350 | / (200 + 350) / 2)) * 100

= (150 / 275) * 100

= 54.54%

Percentage difference

= (| 10-12 | / (10 + 12) / 2)) * 100

= 18.18%

Note: Ignore the minus sign if the result is negative. Many people make the mistake of assuming that percentage change and percentage difference are the same thing. As I have just demonstrated, they are not.

We use percentage change when there is an old value and a new value and we need to know the percentage of rise or fall in relation to the old value. Most of the time we use percentage change in reporting.

Percentage error

This metric is used to calculate the percentage of magnitude of the error when comparing approximate value to an exact value.

Percentage error

= (| approximate value – exact value | / | exact value |) * 100

For example:

	Approximate conversions	Actual conversions	% error
July	200	110	81.82%
Aug	300	200	50%

I estimated 200 conversions in July, but got 110 conversions:

Percentage error

= (| 200 - 110 | / 110) * 100

= 81.82%

I estimated 300 conversions in August, but got 200 conversions:

Percentage error

= (| 300 - 200 | / 200) * 100

= 50%

A practical way that you can use percentage error is when you are running an experiment. You want percentage error to be as low as possible.

Note: Ignore the minus sign if the result is negative.

Percentage points

We use percentage points when we subtract one percentage from another to imply that the change is not relative.

For example, if the conversion rate jumps from 10% to 12%. Do you report a 20% rise in conversion rate or a 2% rise in conversion rate?

It is actually a 20% rise in conversion rate or a 2 percentage point rise in conversion. It cannot be a 2% rise in conversion rate.

Mean

Also known as arithmetic mean or population mean, mean is simply an average of the numbers. Mean is a type of average and is denoted by the Greek letter μ ("mu")

Although average could be mean, median, mode or variance, the mean metric is used a lot in Google Analytics under the name of 'average'. This includes average time on page, average time on site and site averages.

> *Mean*
> *= sum of numbers / count of numbers*

For example, let us imagine a website has got five web pages:

	Bounce Rate
Page 1	35%
Page 2	40%
Page 3	0%
Page 4	48%
Page 5	100%

If we calculate the bounce rate of the site:

Bounce rate

= (35 + 40 + 0 + 48 + 100) / 5

= 223 / 5

= 44.6%

Is 44.6% a true bounce rate? No.

Look at the distribution of bounce rate across all the web pages. Two web pages, page 3 and page 5 have extreme values of 0% and 100%. We call such values as **outliers** in statistics and as we already know outliers have the sadistic ability to skew averages.

If we take out these two extreme values from our calculations then we can get more accurate bounce rate of the site:

Bounce rate

= (35 + 40 + 48) / 3

= 123 / 3

= 41%

Let's look at another similar example:

	Average time on page (in seconds)
Page 1	350
Page 2	400
Page 3	500
Page 4	480
Page 5	36000

Average time on the website

= (350 + 400 + 500 + 480 + 36000) / 5

= 37730 / 5

= 7546

= 2 hrs 6 minutes

Again the outlier '36000' is skewing our average metric. If we take it out and then re-calculate the average time on site:

Average time on the website

= (350 + 400 + 500 + 480) / 4

= 1730 / 4

= 432.5

= 7 minutes 12 seconds

Therefore whenever we analyse 'average' metrics we always:

- Look at the distribution.
- Identify the outliers (i.e. extreme values).
- **Discount outliers** from the averages' calculations.

If you do not do this then you will get **muddy analytical insight** from your average metrics, for example, the average time on the site is calculated as 2hrs 6 minutes.

Unit price

Unit price

= cost / quantity

Tell me, out of the following which do you think is a better deal?

- Placement of three ads for $40.12.
- Placement of two ads for $30.65.

Calculating and comparing unit prices is a good way of finding the best deal.

If we calculate the unit price in each case:

Three ads

= $40.12 / 3

= $13.37 per ad

Two ads

= $30.65 / 2

= $15.32 per ad

So if we go for the 'two ads for $30.65' deal we will end up paying more. Consequently, the best deal for us is 'three ads for $40.12'.

Profit

There are many types of profit; gross profit, operating profit, net profit, bottom-line profit etc.

Lot of marketers make the mistake of reporting these metrics without understanding what these metrics really are and how they are calculated.

In simple terms:

Profit = sales − cost

*Revenue = price of the product(s) * quantity sold*

Gross profit = sales − direct cost

Direct cost could include the cost of manufacturing a product.

Operating profit = sales − operating cost

Operating profit is calculated before interest and taxes. Operating cost is the ongoing cost of running a business, product or system. It can include both direct and indirect costs.

Net profit = sales − total cost

Total cost could include any direct and indirect costs plus interest plus taxes.

Net Profit, also known as net income, net earnings or bottom-line, is the profit after interest and taxes.

When we talk about a business's bottom-line, we are actually talking about **net profit.**

Profit margin

Profit margin is also known as net profit margin, net margin and net profit ratio.

*Profit margin = (net profit/revenue) * 100*

A low profit margin means a higher risk. A decline in sales will erase the profit and result in a net loss.

Lesson 17: Key performance indicators (KPI)

What is a KPI?

Key performance indicators (KPI) are metrics used to determine how you are performing against your business objectives.

A metric can be a number or a ratio. So we have number metrics and we have ratio metrics.

For example, visits (or sessions), pageviews, revenue etc. are **number metrics** because they are in the form of numbers. Bounce rate, conversion rate, average order value etc. are **ratio metrics** because they are in the form of ratios.

"Because KPI are also metrics, we can have KPI in the form of both numbers and ratios. We can have number KPI and we can have ratio KPI."

For example:

- Days to purchase, visits to purchase, revenue etc. are **number KPI**.
- Conversion rate, average order value, task completion rate etc. are **ratio KPI**.

The difference between a metric and KPI

"A metric graduates to a KPI."

In order for a metric to graduate to a KPI the metric must **massively impact the business bottom-line**.

This is possible only when the metric has the ability to provide recommendation(s) for action which can have a huge impact on the business bottom-line.

> *"Your KPI must have the ability to provide recommendation(s) for action which can hugely impact the business bottom-line."*

For example, average order value can be used as a KPI because it hugely impacts the business bottom-line. You can greatly increase sales at the present conversion rate just by increasing the size of the orders.

Revenue per click, revenue per visit, revenue per acquisition, cost per acquisition, task completion rate etc. are other examples of metrics which can be used as KPI.

How to find a good KPI?

Before you start the process of finding KPI, you must acquire a very good understanding of your business and its objectives. Then you need to translate your business objectives into measurable goals.

Once you have determined your goals, you will select KPI for each of these goals. You will use these KPI to measure the performance of each goal.

> *"Goals are specific strategies you used to achieve your business objectives."*

Your business objective could be **increase sales**.

Your goal could be something like **increase sales by 5% in the next three months by increasing the average order value from X to 2X.**

"Any metric which has the ability to directly impact the cash flow (revenue, cost) and/or conversions (both macro and micro conversions) in a big way can be a good KPI."

For example, if you sell display banner ad space on your website and display advertising is the main source of revenue for you then pageviews can be used as a KPI. The more pageviews you get, the more you can charge for every thousand impressions (known as Cost per Thousand (CPM)) from your advertisers.

If you are not sure whether or not a metric can be used as a KPI, then try to correlate it with revenue, cost and/or conversions over a period of time (three or more months).

You need to prove that there is a linear relationship between your chosen KPI and revenue, cost and/or conversions i.e. as the value of your KPI increases or decreases there is a corresponding increase or decrease in revenue, cost and/or conversions.

Can you use number of Twitter followers as a KPI?

The answer is no, not unless you can correlate the number of Twitter followers with revenue, cost and/or conversions i.e. as the number of Twitter followers increases or decreases there is a corresponding increase or decrease in revenue, cost and/or conversions.

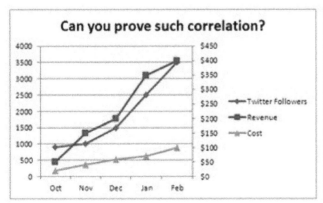
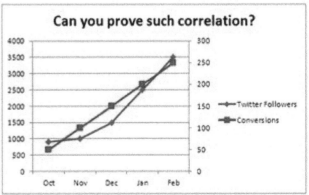

Even if somehow you are able to correlate the number of Twitter followers with revenue, cost and/or conversions you still need to prove that the correlation has a **huge impact** on the business bottom-line.

> *"Just because a metric impacts the business bottom-line, does not automatically make it a good KPI."*

Can you use number of Facebook fans as a KPI?

The answer is no, not unless you can correlate the number of Facebook fans with revenue, cost and/or conversions i.e. as the number of Facebook fans increases or decreases there is a corresponding increase or decrease in revenue, cost and/or conversions.

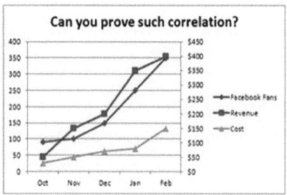 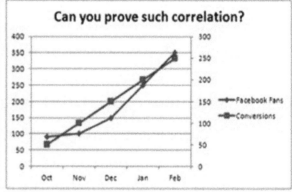

Even if somehow you are able to correlate the number of Facebook fans with revenue, cost and/or conversions you still need to prove that the number of Facebook fans has a **huge impact** on the business bottom-line.

Can you use phone calls as a KPI?

The answer is yes, provided the majority of your revenue comes through phone calls. You can easily track phone calls through phone call tracking software and then import the phone call data into Google Analytics.

Once the data is imported you can tie phone calls to revenue, cost and/or conversions to determine correlation.

There is one thing to keep in mind:

"KPI does not need to be a metric available in Google Analytics reports."

You can use metrics from other analytics tools too.

For example phone call metrics are not available in Google Analytics reports by default but this does not mean that we cannot use it as a KPI.

Similarly, the **task completion rate** metric is not available in Google Analytics reports. However you can calculate task completion rate through a survey tool, such as **Qualaroo,** and use it as a KPI.

"Task completion rate is the percentage of people who came to your website and answered 'yes' to the survey question 'were you able to complete the task for which you came to the website?'."

Can you use client happiness as a KPI?

The answer is no, because a KPI is a metric and a metric is a number or a ratio. In other words:

"Metrics are something which can be measured in the first place."

How you can possibly quantify a human emotion such as happiness?

Types of KPI

There are two broad categories of KPI:

1. Internal KPI.
2. External KPI.

Internal KPI

These KPI are internally used by team members to measure and optimize their marketing campaign's performance. They are not always reported to clients/boss/senior management.

"Internal KPI do not need to be business bottom-line impacting."

The following KPIs can be used to measure your link building outreach campaigns:

1. Delivery rate.
2. Open rate.
3. Response rate.
4. Conversion rate of outreach.
5. ROI of outreach.

Often marketers make the terrible mistake of reporting internal KPI to clients/senior management.

For example, bounce rate is a good internal KPI for optimizing landing pages but it is not something which you would report to a CEO. We report only KPI which hugely impact the business bottom-line to senior management.

External KPI

External KPI are the KPI we report to clients/senior management. They are also used to create **web analytics measurement models** (strategic roadmaps) for businesses.

"External KPI must be hugely business bottom-line impacting."

Whenever we talk about KPI in general, we are referring to external KPI.

Here are some examples of external KPI:

1. Average order value.
2. Conversion rate.
3. Revenue.
4. Revenue per acquisition.
5. Cost per acquisition.
6. Task completion rate.
7. Goal conversions.

Note: External KPI can also be used as internal KPI. There are no hard and fast rules here.

Attributes of a good KPI

A good KPI has the following attributes:

1. Available and measurable

You can only use those metrics as KPI which are available to you in the first place. For example, if the net promoter score metric is not available to you then you cannot use it as a KPI.

Similarly if you come up with something which is impossible to measure (such as the frustration level of customers who abandoned the shopping cart for the third time) then you cannot use it is as a KPI.

> *"When you are finding your KPI, you need to be 100% sure that there is a mechanism/tool available out there to measure and report your KPI in the first place."*

2. Has a massive impact on the business bottom-line

If a metric does not greatly impact the business bottom-line then it is not a good external KPI.

3. Relevant

If your KPI has a huge impact on the business bottom-line then it has got to be relevant to your business objectives.

Conversely, if your KPI is not relevant to your business objectives then it cannot be impacting your business bottom-line.

4. Instantly useful

If your KPI has a huge impact on your business bottom-line then it has got to be instantly useful i.e. you can quickly take action on the basis of the insight you get from your KPI.

5. Timely

Your KPI should be available to you in a timely manner so that you can make timely decisions.

For example, if you are using a **compound metric** (a metric which is made up of several other metrics) as a KPI and it takes several months to compute it once and then several more months to compute it for a second time then it is not considered a good KPI as it is not possible to make timely decisions on the basis of such a KPI.

Examples of good KPI

Gross profit

Gross profit is profit after production and manufacturing costs.

Gross profit

= sales revenue – direct costs

Direct costs can include the cost of manufacturing a product.

Gross profit margin

Gross profit margin is used to determine how effective your business is at keeping production costs under control. The higher the gross profit margin, the more money is left over for operating expenses and net profit.

Gross profit margin

*= (gross profit / revenue) * 100*

Operating profit

Operating profit is the profit before interest and taxes.

Operating profit

= sales revenue – operating costs

Operating costs are the ongoing costs of running a business, product or system. They can include both direct and indirect costs.

Operating profit margin

Operating profit margin is used to determine the effectiveness of your business in keeping operating costs under control. The higher the operating profit margin, the more money is left over for net profit.

Operating profit margin

*= (operating profit / revenue) * 100*

Net profit

Also known as net income, net earnings or bottom-linen, net profit is the profit after interest and taxes.

> *Net profit*
> *= sales revenue − total cost*

Total costs include any direct and indirect costs plus interest plus taxes.

Net profit margin

Also known as profit margin, net margin or net profit ratio, net profit margin is used to determine the effectiveness of your business in converting sales into profit.

> *Net profit margin*
> *= (net profit / revenue) * 100*

A low profit margin indicates a higher risk. A decline in sales would erase the profit and result in a net loss.

Revenue growth rate

Also known as sales growth rate, revenue growth rate is the measure of the percentage increase in sales between two time periods.

> *Revenue growth rate*
> *= (current month's revenue − previous months revenue) / (previous month's revenue) * 100*

Total economic value

Total economic value is the total value added by your product/service/campaigns to the business bottom-line. It also takes into account the role played by micro conversions and conversions which assisted and completed the sales.

> *Total economic value*
> *= total revenue + total value of the assisting conversions + total value of the last click conversions*

Return on investment (ROI)

ROI is used to evaluate the efficiency of your investment or to compare the efficiency of different investments.

> *Return on investment*
> *= (gain from investment – cost of investment)/cost of investment*

Net promoter score

Net promoter score tells you how likely it is that your customers will recommend your business to a friend or colleague.

> *Net promoter score*
> *= percentage of promoters – percentage of detractors*

Customer lifetime value

Customer lifetime value is the projected revenue a customer will generated during his lifetime (repeat business). Different types of customers have a different **lifetime value (LTV)**.

One of the best ways to boost LTV is by improving customer satisfaction.

Customer lifetime value

= average order value * number of repeat transactions * average customer life span in months or years

The average customer life span is how long they remain your customer.

Customer retention rate

Customer retention rate is used to determine how good your company is in retaining customers.

Customer retention rate

= (1- (customers lost in a given time period/total number of customers acquired in the same time period)) * 100

Customer profitability score

Customer profitability score is used to separate profitable customers from unprofitable customers.

Customer profitability score

= revenue earned through a customer – cost associated with customers management/service/retention

Cost per lead

Cost per lead is the average cost of generating a lead.

Cost per lead

= total cost / total leads

Cost per acquisition

Cost per acquisition is the average cost of acquiring a customer or generating a conversion.

Cost per acquisition
= total cost / total acquisitions

Revenue per acquisition

Revenue per acquisition is the average revenue earned through an acquisition.

Revenue per acquisition
= total revenue / total acquisitions

Per visit value

Per visit value is the average value of a visit to your website.

Per visit value
= total revenue / total visits

Conversion rate

Conversion rate is the percentage of visits which results in goal conversions or ecommerce transactions.

Conversion rate
*= (total goal conversions / total visits) * 100*

Average order value

Average order value is the average value of an ecommerce transaction. Through this metric you can measure how effective your upselling and cross selling efforts are and whether you are helping people to find the product they are looking for.

Average order value

= total revenue / total ecommerce transactions

Task completion rate

Task completion rate is the percentage of people who came to your website and answered 'yes' to the following survey question - Were you able to complete the task for which you came to the website?

Task completion rate

= (number of people said 'yes' to the survey question / total number of survey responses) * 100

There is virtually no limit to the number of good KPI you can find. It all depends upon the nature of your business and the industry you work in.

For example, if you work in an industry where the majority or all of the conversions occur via phone calls then you can use phone calls as your KPI.

Solve for your customers and not for your KPI

We often hear goals such as "we want to improve conversion rate by X" or "we want to increase traffic by Y" from marketers and business owners. While nothing really is wrong with these goals, they are simply not agile.

You cannot rapidly deploy solutions with these types of goals.

For example, imagine that you want to improve the conversion rate of your website.

Now you have no idea how to do that without some deep data analysis. You are not sure where to start, which report(s) to look at or which report(s) to overlook.

So you start your analysis. You go through report after report looking for anomalies and trying to find something which may need fixing. You have no idea where your analysis is going to take you and how long it is going to take.

But you have to find a solution, so you segment and analyze the data. You repeat this process over and over again until you find something which needs fixing. This process is very time consuming and certainly will not lead you to make timely decisions.

Now try to solve the same conversion problem, but another way.

Instead of focusing on your KPI, focus on solving your customers' problems one at a time. For example, through customer feedback, you find out that there is a technical problem with your shopping cart which is causing your customers to abandon the purchase.

Now you know the problem all you have to do is go ahead and recommend fixing this problem ASAP. Once you fix your customers' problem, your conversion rate is going to increase regardless of whether or not you structure your entire work around improving this metric.

You could have resolved the issue by focusing on your KPI but it would have taken you much longer to find and fix the same problem.

Since data driven marketers tend not to look beyond data, they remain busy chasing KPI such as conversion rate – "We have to improve conversion rate by X" or "we have to improve sales by Y".

On the other hand, data smart marketers look beyond data and do not go around chasing KPI. They focus on solving their customers' problems, one at a time.

We all need to be data smart.

Lesson 18: Selecting the best Excel charts for data analysis and reporting

Do you always struggle to know which type of Excel charts to use in your analytics reports?

The type of Excel chart you select for your analysis and reporting depends upon what you are going to analyse and report.

We create charts to display qualitative and quantitative data in a graphical format and to make it easy to understand either one, any or all of the following:

1. Type of data (qualitative and quantitative).
2. Relationship among data.
3. Comparison of data.
4. Composition of data.
5. Distribution of data.
6. Overlapping of data.

Understanding qualitative and quantitative data

Qualitative data is the data that can be classified/categorized but it cannot be measured. For example, colours, satisfaction, rankings etc.

Quantitative data (also known as interval/ratio data) is the data that can be measured. For example, number of customers, number of steps, conversion rate, height etc.

Types of qualitative data

Types of qualitative data include nominal data and ordinal data.

Nominal data

Qualitative data that cannot be put into a meaningful order (i.e. ranked) is classed as nominal data. For example {Blue, Yellow, Green, Red, Black}.

Ordinal data

Qualitative data that can be put into a meaningful order (i.e. ranked) is ordinal data. For example {very satisfied, satisfied, unsatisfied, very unsatisfied} or {strong dislike, dislike, neutral, like, strong like}.

Types of quantitative data

Types of quantitative data include discrete data and continuous data.

Discrete data

Discrete data is quantitative data with distinct values/observations. For example 5 customers, 17 points, 12 steps etc.

Continuous data

Continuous data is quantitative data with any value/observation within a finite or infinite interval. For example conversion rate, visits, pageviews, bounce rate, height, weight etc.

How to summarize qualitative data

You can summarize qualitative data in a number of ways.

Using a frequency table:

Observation	Frequency (%)
Blue	40.00%
Yellow	10.00%
Green	5.00%
Red	20.00%
Black	25.00%

Using a pie chart:

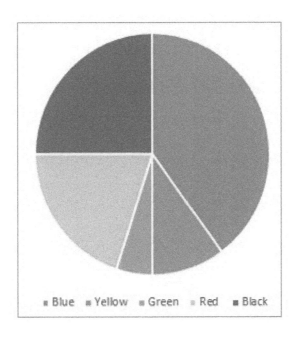

■ Blue ■ Yellow ■ Green ■ Red ■ Black

Using a column chart:

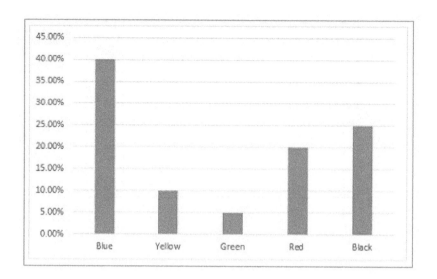

How not to summarize qualitative data

You cannot summarize qualitative data by calculating the mean (or average).

For example:

Very satisfied: 40%

Satisfied: 30%

Unsatisfied: 20%

Very unsatisfied: 10%

When you calculate the average for the above results the average satisfaction is 25%, which does not make any sense.

Look at it this way, when you are attempting to calculate the average of qualitative data, you are actually trying to do the following:

Average satisfaction

= (very satisfied + satisfied + unsatisfied + very unsatisfied) / 4

This is not possible as you cannot quantify satisfaction, it is a feeling.

Similarly, you cannot summarize qualitative data using line charts and histograms.

Ways to summarize quantitative data

You can summarize quantitative data using mean, median, mode, standard deviation etc.

You can summarize quantitative data using column charts, bar charts, line charts, histograms etc.

Relationships among data

To understand relationships, you need to understand the connection/correlation between two or more **data points**.

A data point/category is a mark on a graph/chart which corresponds to a piece of data.

The data that the mark represents is also called a data point.

The value associated with a data point is called the data value.

A variable can store one or more data values which we can represent graphically via a chart.

A set of related data points is known as a data series.

For example, the following chart has 15 data points and two data series:

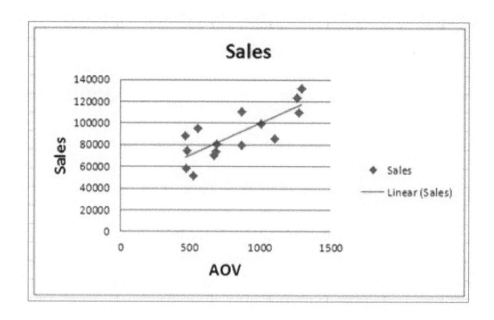

Here we are trying to understand the relationship between two variables named 'average order value' and 'sales'. One of the best Excel charts to use to represent this relationship is a **scatter chart**.

We can see from the chart that the relationship between the two variables is linear which means as the value of average order value (AOV) increases there is a corresponding increase in the value of sales.

Consider using scatter chart when:

1. Analysing and reporting the relationship/correlation between two variables.

2. When you want to show 'why'. For example: why revenue is correlated with average order value or why the conversion rate is correlated with number of transactions.

3. When there are more than ten data points on the horizontal axis. The more data points the better for a scatter chart. Conversely, fewer data points (e.g. five or six data points) are not good enough for creating a scatter chart.

4. There are two variables that depend on each other.

Comparison of data

For comparing two or more variables the best charts are **column charts**, **bar charts**, **line charts** and **combination charts.**

Column charts

Column charts are one of the most widely used charts and are a frequently used to compare variables.

In column charts categories are plotted along the horizontal axis and values are plotted along the vertical axis.

For example, the following column chart compares the performance of the number of branded keywords and the number of non-branded keywords which generated traffic on the website between July and November.

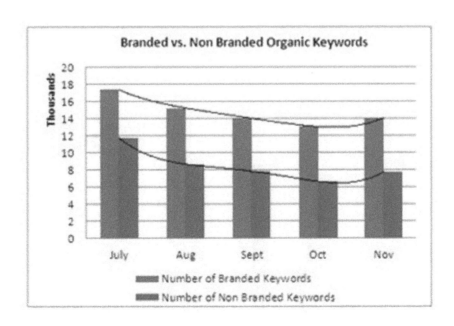

Here the categories (number of branded keywords, number of non-branded keywords) are plotted on the horizontal axis whilst their values are plotted on the vertical axis.

Here are some examples of columns charts that you should avoid creating.

Avoid comparing two variables through a column chart that have different units of measurement:

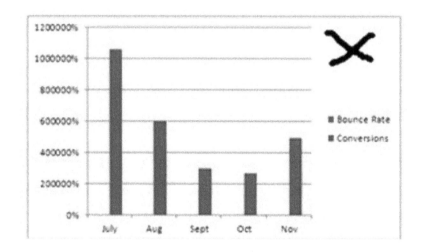

Avoid comparing two variables where the values of one variable completely dwarfs the values of the other variable:

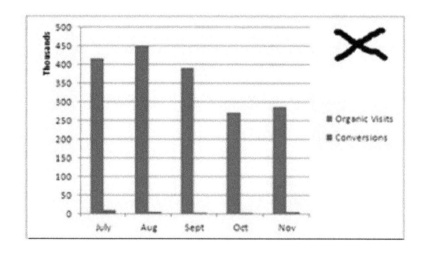

Avoid plotting too many categories as it creates clutter and makes the chart hard to read:

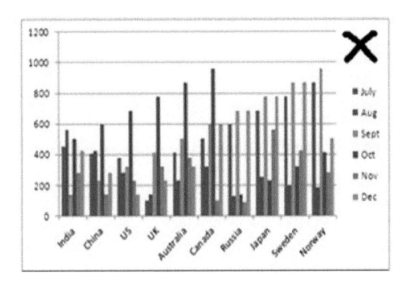

Avoid using a column chart when the axis labels are long. Instead use a horizontal bar chart:

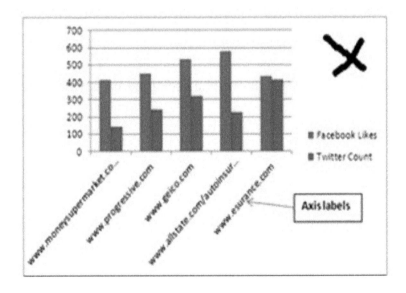

Consider using column charts when:

1. You are comparing two or more variables which have the same unit of measurement and are of comparable sizes. This ensures that the values of one variable do not dwarf the values of the other variables.

2. When you want to show 'how much'. For example how much have organic visits changed over the past three months. Column charts are good for showing data changes over a period of time.

3. The number of categories to plot is less than five.

4. You want to show maximum and minimum values.

Bar charts

Bar charts are similar to column charts except that values in bar charts are plotted horizontally and categories are plotted vertically.

For example, the following bar chart shows the social media performance of various insurance websites:

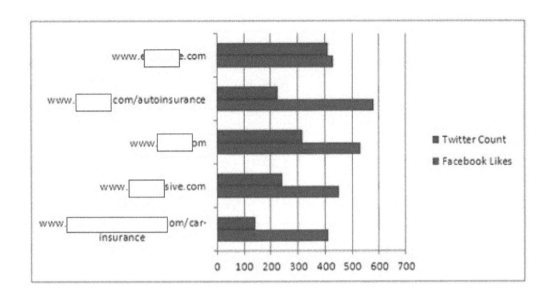

As you can see here the categories (website names) are plotted on the vertical axis and values are plotted on the horizontal axis.

Consider using bar charts when:

1. The axis labels are too long to fit on a column chart.

2. The number of categories to plot is between five and eight.

3. You are comparing two or more variables which have same unit of measurement and are of comparable sizes.

4. You want to show 'how much'.

5. You want to show maximum and minimum values.

Line charts

Line charts are best used to show data trends, especially over a long period of time. For example, the following line chart shows the performance of organic and PPC traffic between July and March.

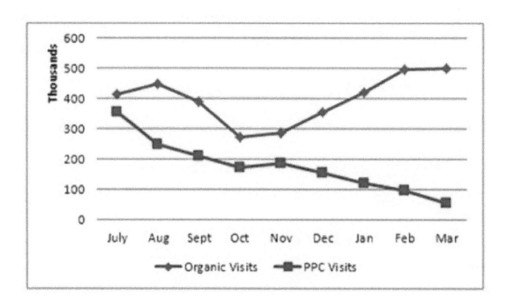

Another example:

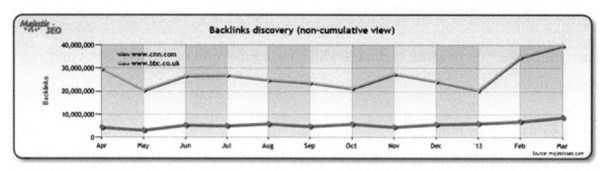

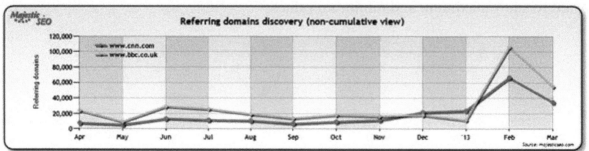

In this example I am visualizing the link growth/velocity of the BBC and CNN websites during the last year using the Majestic Back Links History Tool.

I have used a line chart because they are too many data points to plot and because I want to show the data trend over a long period of time.

Another example:

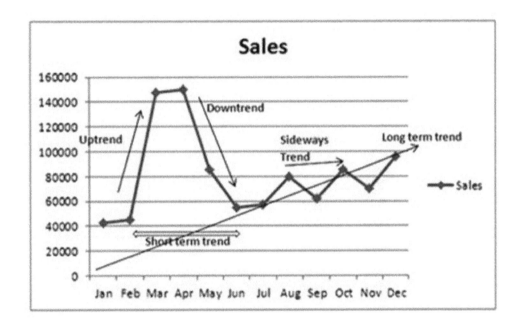

Line charts are best used to show data trends including uptrend, downtrend, short term trend, sideways trend and long term trend.

Consider using line charts when:

1. You want to show data trends over a long period of time.

2. The number of categories to plot is more than eight.

3. You have too many data points to plot and the column or bar chart clutters the data.

4. You want to show 'how much' has changed over a period of time.

Combination charts

A combination chart is a combination of two or more charts. For example a combination of a column chart with a line chart.

Consider using a combination chart when you are comparing two or more variables that have different units of measurement and/or are of different sizes.

For example:

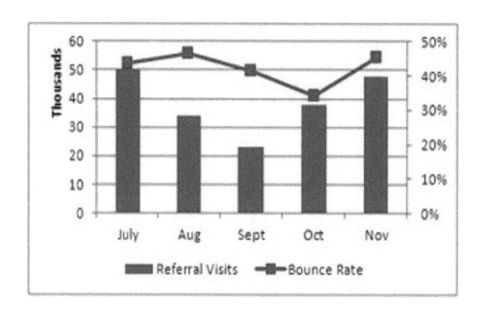

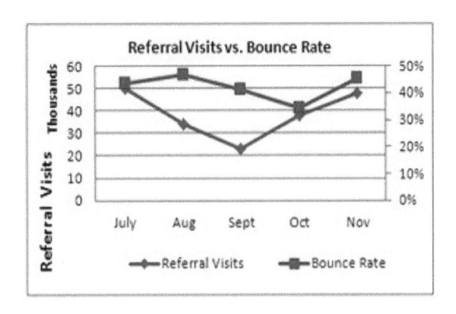

Here both of the combination charts are presenting the same data.

The only difference is that, in the first chart I combined the column chart with a line chart. In the second chart I just plotted the bounce rate on a secondary axis.

I use combination charts a lot in my reports and it is important that you know how to create them because they are very useful.

Please note: By using a combination chart you can ensure that the value of one variable does not dwarf the value of the other variable(s).

Composition of data

If you want to show the breakdown of data into its constituents then consider using a **pie chart, stacked column chart** or **stacked area chart**.

Pie charts

Pie charts are most useful when you have only one data series, less than five categories/data points to plot and you want to show composition of data.

For example, the following pie chart shows the breakdown of my website traffic sources in the last one month:

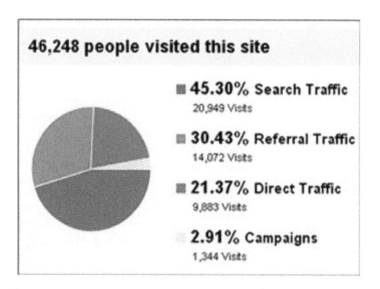

Here I have got only four categories (search traffic, referral traffic, direct traffic and campaigns) to plot. So a pie chart is ideal to show the breakdown.

If there were more than four categories to plot (such as eight or ten categories) then the pie chart becomes cluttered and hard to read.

Another example:

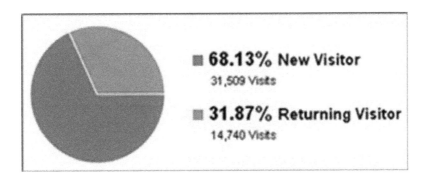

Here we have got only two categories to plot (new visitors and returning visitors) so the use of a pie chart to show data composition is ideal.

Following are some pie charts that you should avoid creating.

Too many categories make this pie chart hard to read and understand:

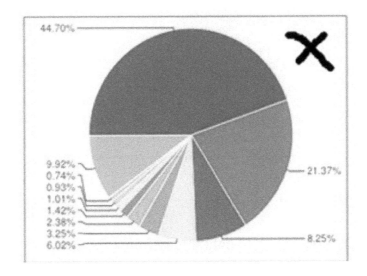

Avoid using pie charts when the categories do not represent parts of the whole pie:

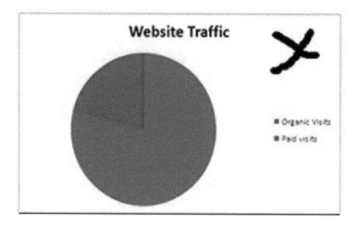

Avoid using a pie chart if the value of one variable completely dwarfs the value of other variables or some valuables are zero or negative:

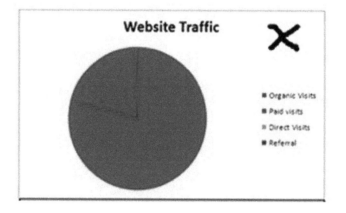

Consider using pie charts when:

1. You want to show the breakdown of data into its constituents.

2. You have only one data series.

3. You have less than five data points to plot.

4. The data points represent the parts of the whole pie.

5. The constituents are of comparable sizes so that value of one constituent does not dwarf the values of other constituents.

Stacked column charts

Stacked column charts are most useful when you have five to eight categories/data points to plot and you want to show the composition of data.

For example, the following stacked column chart shows the breakdown of website traffic in terms of new and returning visits in the last month:

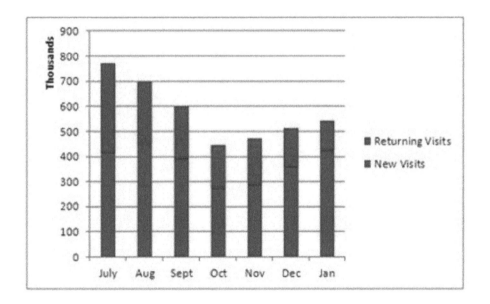

Consider using a stacked column chart when:

1. You want to show the breakdown of data into its constituents.

2. You have between five to eight data points to plot.

3. The data points represent the parts of the whole composition.

4. The constituents are of comparable sizes so that the value of one constituent does not dwarf the values of the other constituents.

Stacked area charts

Stacked area charts are most useful when you have more than eight categories/data points to plot and you want to show the **trend of composition**.

For example, the following stacked area chart shows the breakdown of website traffic:

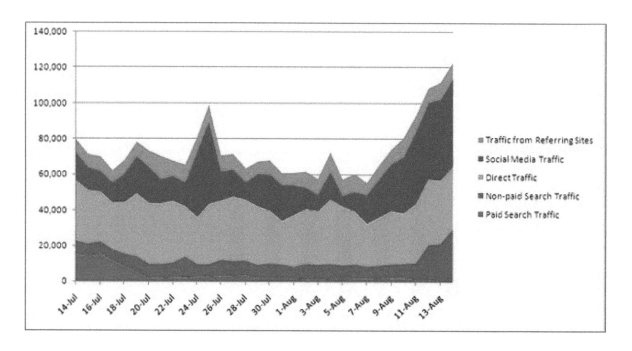

Consider using a stacked area chart when:

1. You want to show the trend of composition.

2. You want to emphasize the magnitude of change over time.

3. You have more than eight data points to plot.

4. The data points represent the parts of the whole composition.

218

5. The constituents are of comparable sizes so that the value of one constituent does not dwarf the values of the other constituents.

Distribution of data

If you want to show distribution of data then consider using a **column chart, bar chart, scatter chart** or **histogram**.

We need to determine the distribution of data points (i.e. how narrow or wide spread the distribution is) in order to trust the **average metrics**.

If the distribution is widespread then the average value is not a true representative of the typical value in a data set and hence we cannot trust the average metrics.

One of the best charts to show distribution of data is a histogram:

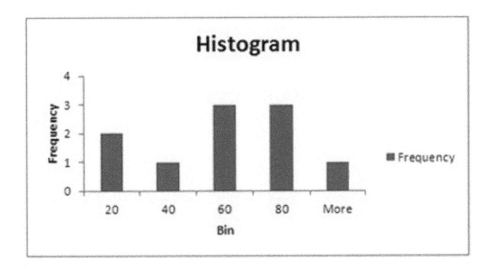

Please note: You will need to install the '**Analysis ToolPak**' in order to create histograms in Excel.

Overlapping of data

If you want to show 'overlapping of data' then consider using Venn diagrams.

The **multi-channel conversion visualizer chart** used in Google Analytics to visualize multi-channel attribution is actually a Venn diagram:

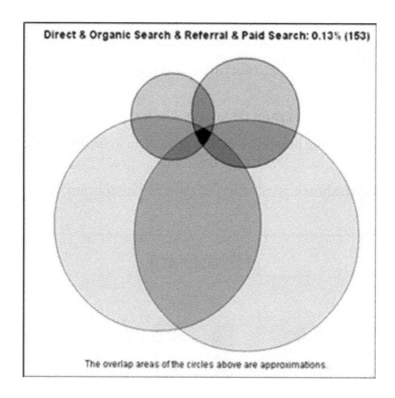

We can use a Venn diagram to determine whether or not a website has got an attribution problem.

If there is little to no overlap between two or more marketing channels then the website does not have attribution issues.

If there is a good amount of overlap then the website has got attribution issues and you should seriously consider taking multi-channel attribution into account while analysing and interpreting the performance of marketing campaigns.

Another great use of Venn diagrams is in visualizing the back links overlaps between websites:

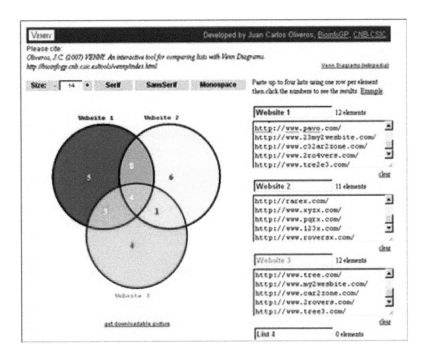

The tool that I have used to create this Venn diagram is known as Venny.

Please note: You can create a Venn diagram in Excel. There is a good tutorial on the Microsoft Office website.

Adding context to your chart

Different people will analyse and interpret the same chart differently. It all depends upon the **context** in which they analyse and interpret the chart.

No matter what chart you select, some people will always find a way to misinterpret your chart. Therefore it is critical that you **provide context with your chart** in the form of written commentary which exactly describes the intent of your chart.

First present the context, then the insight, then the chart to support your insight.

In this way you are giving clues to your chart reader regarding how to read your chart.

For example:

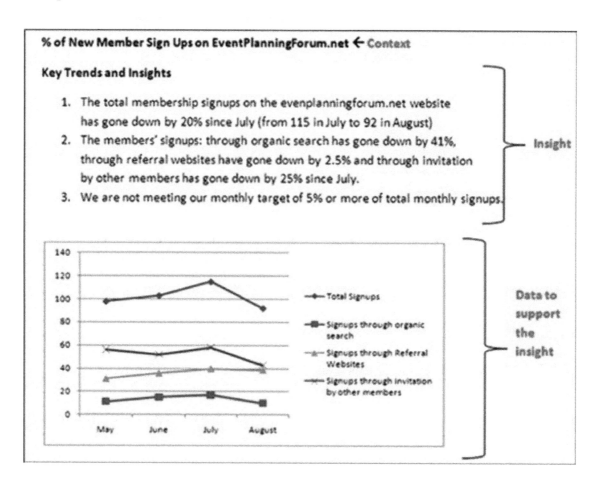

Charts to avoid for reporting purposes

There are some charts which are worth mentioning to you because they should be avoided at all costs:

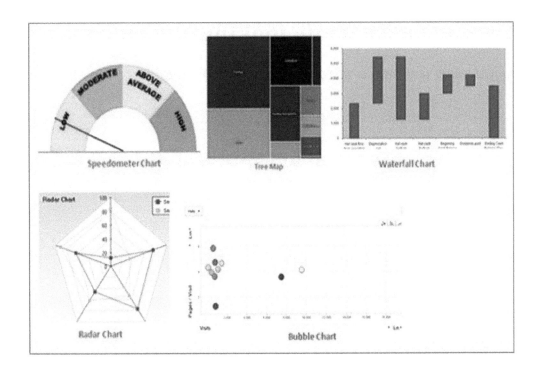

The reason that you should avoid reporting data to your clients via these charts is simple. The majority of people have no idea what you are trying to communicate via these charts.

The speedometer chart looks so unprofessional, yet many marketers use them in reports. The tree map looks like an aerial view of an open field with marked territories (this is the opinion of one of my clients).

The waterfall chart looks like there has been a misprint of a column chart (another feedback from one of my clients). Nobody understands radar charts or bubble charts. I have yet to see any good uses of bubble charts (a.k.a. motion charts) in Google Analytics.

Use these charts only when your target audience is as data savvy as you.

Use common sense while looking at a chart

Sometimes just using common sense does the trick. For example:

Is Global warming real?

59% - somewhat likely

35% - very likely

26% - not very likely

How reliable is this analysis if the numbers do not add up to 100%?

Here is another chart:

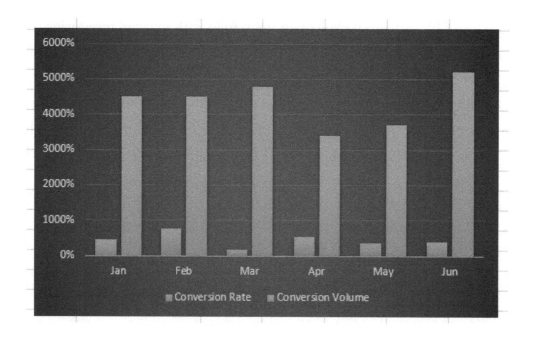

What is wrong with this chart? Well, you cannot compare conversion rate and conversion volume in this way because they both have different units of measurement.

Takeaways

- Do not blindly believe whatever a chart is telling you.
- Look at the charts closely. Look for truncated y axis, missing scales, the number of data points plotted and variable types.
- Do the basic maths and question the data if something does not seem right.

Part two:
Statistics for web analytics and conversion optimization

Lesson 1: Introduction to statistics for web analytics and conversion optimization

The role of statistics in the world of web analytics is not clear to many marketers. Not many talk or write about the usage of statistics and data science in web analytics.

Unfortunately, by and large, the analytics industry is still dominated by data collection methodologies and tools. We are all obsessed with collecting more data. Lot of different type of data. But rarely do we focus on analysing and interpreting the data we already have.

For example, someone may learn a new hack about collecting a particular type of data and then he/she blogs about it in the name of analytics. Then there are the people who talk about Excel hacks in the name of analytics. But neither Excel hacks nor data collection tips and tricks will improve your business bottom-line.

What will really improve your business bottom-line is the accurate interpretation of the data along with the actions you take on the basis of that interpretation.

Only by leveraging the knowledge of statistics and understanding the context, can you accurately interpret data and take actions which can improve your business bottom-line.

I spent an awful lot of time reading books and articles on statistics and data science in a hope that I will find something which might help me in my career.

I must admit that the majority of topics I read on statistics initially do not seem to have anything directly to do with my job.

This could be one reason why statistics is not taken seriously in the internet marketing industry. But overall, statistics knowledge has improved my interpretation of data. I am constantly looking for new ways to implement statistics in web analytics.

In order to become above average in marketing and/or analytics, you need to learn even more statistics.

> *"Analysing data without a basic understanding of statistics will almost always result in erroneous conclusions. "*

I cannot stress enough the importance of statistics and its supersets **econometrics** and **data science** in solving real life problems. Let me give you one good example.

According to the **law of diminishing marginal utility:**

> *"The first unit of consumption of a good / service produces more utility than second and subsequent units."*

Which means the very first article that you will read on a topic, for example, 'A/B testing best practices' will produce more benefit than the second and subsequent articles on the same topic.

So the more articles you will read on 'A/B testing best practices', the less you will benefit from it. Soon you will reach the point of diminishing returns and once you have crossed this point, your efficiency will start decreasing and you will be less productive.

Needless to say, in the online marketing industry every new shiny thing/topic (from Pinterest, Google Authorship to A/B testing) is tortured to death in the name of blogging and thought leadership and we tend to read every new article on the same topic in a hope to gain something new.

But at the same time we forget, how the law of diminishing marginal utility is making us less and less productive with each additional unit of consumption.

I will explain some of the most useful statistics terms and concepts one by one and will also show you their practical use in web analytics so that you can take advantage of them straightaway.

Lesson 2: Statistical inference

Statistical inference (or statistical conclusion) is the process of drawing conclusion from the data which is subject to random variation.

Observational error is an example of statistical inference.

For example, consider the performance of three campaigns A, B and C in the last one month.

	E-Commerce Conversion Rate
Campaign A	8.25%
Campaign B	19.25%
Campaign C	5.24%

Here campaign B seems to have the highest conversion rate.

Does that mean, campaign B is performing better than campaign A and campaign C?

The answer is we do not know that for sure. This is because here we are assuming that campaign B has highest conversion rate only on the basis of our **observation**.

There could be an observational error. Our assumption could be wrong.

> *Observational error is the difference between the collected data and the actual data.*

In order to minimize observational error, we need to segment the ecommerce conversion rate into visits and transactions:

	Visits	Transactions	E-Commerce Conversion Rate
Campaign A	1820	150	8.25%
Campaign B	20	4	19.25%
Campaign C	780	41	5.24%

Now we know that campaign B does not have the highest conversion rate as its sample size is too small. I will explain sample size later in this book.

Lesson 3: Population and sub-population

Statistical inferences are often drawn from random sample taken from a set of entities (values, potential measurements). This set of entities is known as **population or statistical population**.

Population is a set of entities from which statistical inference is drawn.

	E-Commerce Conversion Rate
Campaign A	8.25%
Campaign B	19.25%
Campaign C	5.24%

The set of campaigns above is an examples of statistical population from which statistical inferences (like which is the highest performing campaign) are drawn.

The subset of statistical population is called sub population.

If you consider a PPC campaign as statistical population then its ad groups can be considered as sub populations.

To understand the properties of statistical population, statisticians first separate the population into distinct sub populations (provided they have distinct properties) and then they try to understand the properties of individual sub-populations.

For the same reason, analytics experts recommend to segment analytics data before you draw statistical inferences from it. So if you want to understand the performance of a PPC campaign, then you need to understand the performance of its individual ad groups.

Similarly if you want to understand the performance of an ad group, then you need to understand the performance of the keywords and ad copies in that ad group.

I hope it is now clear why data segmentation is so important in web analytics.

Lesson 4: Understanding samples

Samples

A sample is a subset of the population which represents the entire population.

So analysing the sample should produce similar results to analysing all of the population.

Sampling

Sampling is the selection of a sample to understand the properties of an entire statistical population.

Sampling is carried out to analyse large data sets in a cost efficient manner and in a reasonable amount of time. For example, Google Analytics selects and analyzes only a subset of data from your website traffic to produce reports in a reasonable amount of time.

Bad samples

A bad sample is a subset of the population which is not a good representative of the entire population.

So analysing a bad sample will not produce similar results to analysing all of the population.

As long as the sample is a good representative of all of the data, analysing a subset of data (or sample) gives similar results to analysing all of the data.

But if the selected sample is not a good representative of all of the data or if the selected sample is too small to make accurate estimates then in such cases you can end up drawing wrong conclusions.

High quality sample

A high quality sample is the one which is random, in other words it is free from selection bias.

> *A selection bias is a statistical error which occurs when you select a sample which is not a good representative of all of the website traffic.*

For example, when you select only returning visitors for A/B testing or only the visitors from organic search then the traffic sample that you have selected is not a good representative of all of the website traffic because returning visitors or organic visitors may behave differently than the average visitors to your website.

So if you run A/B tests and the traffic sample is not a good representative of the average visitors to your website then you are not going to get an accurate insight on how your website visitors respond to different landing page variations (unless of course you are running your test only for a particular traffic segment).

In that case launching a winning variation may not result in any real uplift in sales/conversion rate. The launch of a winning variation may in fact lower your conversion rate.

That is why it is important that you select high quality sample for your A/B tests.

Sample size

> *Sample size is the size of the sample* ☺

In statistics, the larger the sample size, the more reliable the estimates and vice versa.

Consider the following three campaigns:

	Visits	Transactions	E-Commerce Conversion Rate
Campaign A	1820	150	8.25%
Campaign B	20	4	19.25%
Campaign C	780	41	5.24%

Here campaign B does not have the highest conversion rate because its sample size is too small. Just 4 transactions out of 20 visits.

Had campaign B received 1 transaction out of 1 visit, its conversion rate would be 100%. Will that make its performance even better? No.

Since the sample size of campaign B is very small, its conversion rate is not statistically significant (i.e. statistically meaningful).

Decide your sample size in advance in case of A/B test

If you keep running A/B tests while selecting the sample size as you go, you will at some point get statistically significant results even if the control and variation are exactly the same.

This happens because of **repeated significance testing error** in which your test increases its chances of getting false positive results.

A false positive result is a positive test result which is more likely to be false than true.

For example your A/B test finds the difference between control and variation when the difference does not actually exist.

So what you need to do is decide your sample size in advance before you start the test. There are lot of sample size calculators available out there.

Pick one and calculate the sample size you need for your A/B test in advance. To avoid getting false positive test results, stop your test as soon as you have reached your predetermined sample size.

Lesson 5: Data sampling issues

If you see a notification like the one below, in your Google Analytics reports (it does not matter whether it is GA standard or GA Premium), you should immediately stop assuming that you are going to get any accurate data from your report:

This report is based on 484,154 visits (2.64% of visits). Learn more

There is a high probability that reported metrics from 'conversion rate', 'revenue' to 'sessions' could be anywhere from **10% to 80% off the mark** as the sample selected by Google Analytics for its analysis would be a **bad sample** (one which does not represent the entire population/traffic on your website).

So for example Google Analytics may report your last month revenue to be say $2 million when in fact it is only $900k.

Such inaccuracies in data occur because of **bad data sampling**.

You cannot make business and marketing decisions from an analytics report which is based on just 2.64% of the website total visits. You need to minimize data sampling issues as much as possible before you interpret your data.

Your Google Analytics metrics, from sessions, revenue, transactions to ecommerce conversion rate, depend upon the size of the traffic-data sample being analysed by Google.

This means if you change the size of the data sample being analysed, your ecommerce conversion rate could change, the revenue reported by Google Analytics report could change.

You can change the sampling size in the Google Analytics report to adjust it for accuracy and speed, by clicking the drop down menu at the top right hand side and then selecting the option 'Faster response, less precision':

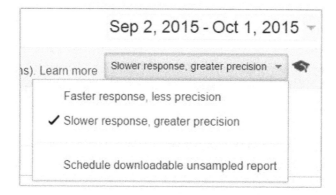

Google Analytics selects only a subset of data (called a sample) from your website traffic to produce reports. This process is known as data sampling.

Sampling is widely used in statistical analysis to analyse large data sets in a cost efficient manner and in a reasonable amount of time. This is why Google Analytics does data sampling.

Google Analytics has an upward limit on the amount of traffic data it will sample to produce reports. This limit has been set to save resources (computation power and cost).

When Google Analytics is sampling your data badly, you cannot rely on the metrics reported by it.

Any marketing decisions based on such reports could result in huge monetary losses.

In the following cases, Google Analytics starts sampling the data when calculating the result for a report:

1. Whenever you apply an advanced segment or a secondary dimension to a Google Analytics report.

2. Whenever you view/request a report that is based on more than 250,000 sessions.

3. Whenever you view/request a multi-channel funnel report which has got more than 1 million conversions.

4. Whenever you view/request a flow visualization report (users flow and goal flow) that is based on more than 100k sessions.

5. Whenever you query for data that is not available in aggregate. This is quite common in the case of custom reports. So whenever you are using custom reports in Google Analytics, the data is being sampled.

How can you determine whether you are viewing a sampled report in Google Analytics?

If you are viewing an un-sampled report in GA then you will see following message at the top of a report: "This report is based on ..... (100% of sessions):

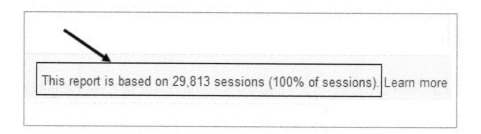

This report is based on 29,813 sessions (100% of sessions). Learn more

However if you are viewing a sampled report then you will see following message at the top of a report: "This report is based on ..... (less than 100% of sessions):

This report is based on 476,353 sessions (4.58% of sessions). Learn more

If your report is based on less than 100% of sessions than you have got data sampling issues. The lower the sample size, the greater the data sampling issue.

For example, a report which is based on 45% of sessions has lower data sampling issues than the report which is based on just 4% of sessions.

Note: You can receive sampled data even when are using Google Analytics API.

If you have a low traffic website (less than 250k sessions a month), you get un-sampled data in your standard reports. If you have a high traffic website (more than 250k sessions a month) then Google may start collecting sampled data even for your standard reports.

Sampled data for high traffic websites often result in poor traffic estimates because the data sample is not a good representative of all of the website traffic. In such case you may have to face data sampling issues.

There are two main causes of data sampling issues in Google Analytics:

1. The data sample selected by Google Analytics is too small to make any accurate traffic estimates.

2. The selected sample is not a good representative of all of the data.

Low traffic websites do not generally face data sampling issues. Google Analytics handles 'data sampling' for such websites really well.

It is only for high traffic websites (more than 250k sessions) each month that Google Analytics may end up doing bad data sampling.

Why data sampling can be very damaging for your business

If you have got data sampling issues you are probably a big business and if you are a big business then the majority of your online marketing decisions have to be data driven.

Consequently you need very high accuracy in traffic data. Otherwise as mentioned earlier, your metrics from conversion rate to revenue to sessions could be anywhere from 10% to 80% off the mark.

You can determine such data discrepancies by comparing a sampled report with its un-sampled version and then calculate the percentage of difference between various metrics.

Make sure that the difference is statistically significant before you draw any conclusion.

Note: Google Analytics Premium lets you download un-sampled reports.

Sampling can create a huge difference to your report so you need to be very careful. Any marketing decisions based on inaccurate date could be fatal for your enterprise business health.

Note: You can rely on metrics like sessions and pageviews even with significant data sampling issues. However you cannot rely on ecommerce metrics (like revenue, transactions, ecommerce conversion rate etc.) when you have got significant data sampling issues.

How can you fix data sampling issues in Google Analytics?

You can never truly eliminate the sampling of data. But here is what you can do to minimize the impact of data sampling issues:

1. Always keep the data sampling setting to 'Slower response, greater precision':

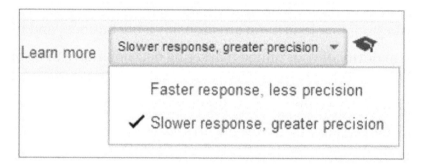

The larger the data size being sampled, the more accurate the traffic estimates.

On the other hand, the smaller the data size being sampled, the less accurate the traffic estimates would be.

But here is one caveat. There is still an upward limit on how big you can make the data sample in Google Analytics.

2. Avoid applying advanced segments or secondary dimensions to your standard reports when you are going to analyse ecommerce metrics like ecommerce conversion rate for reporting purpose and **your analytics account has got data sampling issues.**

3. Run reports for a shorter time frame to include less than 250k sessions. Remember, whenever you view a report that is based on more than 250k sessions Google Analytics automatically start sampling the data.

Download the data and then aggregate it manually.

Note: You cannot aggregate ratio metrics like bounce rate or conversion rate. However you can aggregate number metrics like sessions, pageviews etc.

4. Plan out in advance how you want to segment the data and view the reports. Then instead of applying advanced segments create filtered views/profiles.

The data that is filtered at the view level is generally un-sampled. For standard reports, sampling occurs at the property level and not view level. For multi- channel funnel reports, sampling occurs at the view level and not property level.

For example if you apply the advanced segment 'organic traffic' to the 'all traffic' report so that you can determine the ecommerce conversion rate of your organic search then your report data will be sampled.

But if you create a filtered view which contains only 'organic search data' then your report data could be un-sampled if the requested report is based on less than 250k session.

The best solution to data sampling issues

All of the solutions I have mentioned so far are quick fixes but not permanent solutions for bad data sampling.

If the tips above are not helping much in minimizing data sampling issues then at some point you will have to switch to Google Analytics (GA) Premium or another enterprise level analytics software.

> *You cannot rely on free versions of the analytics tools for large amount of data processing and high accuracy.*

I have been using GA Premium for quite a long time now and I get a lot of emails from people asking about its capabilities and whether a $150k per year spend is really worth it. Here is what I suggest:

> *If your annual online revenue is at least $1 million and your website gets more than 10 million hits/month then you should definitely invest in enterprise level analytics software like GA Premium.*

From my experience it is hard to justify a $150k per year spend on an analytics tool if online revenue is less than $1 million per year.

Google Analytics Premium and data sampling

The data sampling limit of GA Premium is approximately 200 times than that of standard GA which means you get more un-sampled data in GA Premium than in GA standard. GA Premium can handle websites which get 1 billion+ hits per month. So unless you run Google or Yahoo, these data limits should be sufficient for you.

The interface of GA Premium is just like that of standard GA. So for an untrained eye, there is visually no difference between GA Premium and GA standard.

The real difference is in the processing power (besides un-sampled reports). Large data processing and producing un-sampled reports require huge processing loads on the servers which is very costly. I think this is what makes GA Premium so expensive.

If you have got access to GA Premium, you can follow the steps below to get un-sampled reports:

Step 1: Go to the report for which you want an un-sampled data in your GA view.

Step 2: Select 'un-sampled report' from the 'export' drop down menu:

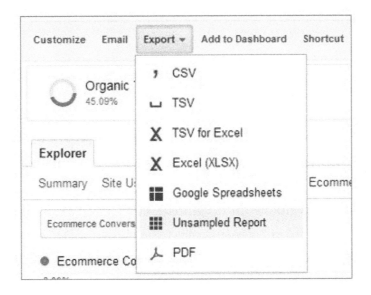

Note: Un-sampled reports are available only in GA Premium.

Step 3: Name the report, select the frequency and click on the 'request un-sampled' button. Here the frequency means how often you want the un-sampled report: once, daily, weekly, monthly or quarterly:

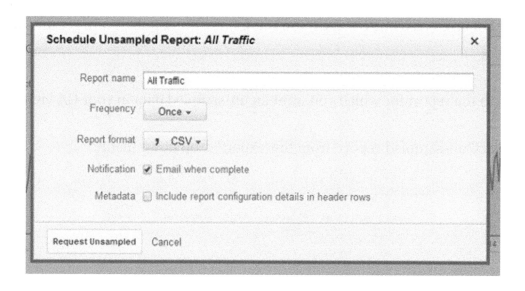

Step 4: Now click on the 'customization' tab, then 'un-sampled reports' to see your requested report and the availability status of the report (pending, completed).

Step 5: Once the report is available for download, click 'csv' to download the report.

One point worth noting here is that, data sampling issues are not limited to just Google Analytics. They can be found everywhere.

Most of the statistics are based on data samples and if you are not sure whether the selected sample is a good representative of all of the data then you could be looking at biased/inaccurate reports and analysis.

For example, say your client sells analytics software called 'XYZ' and he ran a survey in which he asked his clients to select the best analytics software among all the software available on the market.

The majority of his clients are likely to rate 'XYZ' as the best analytics software as they are already paying for it.

The problem with this scenario is the selected sample. Although it is a **representative sample,** it is not random. It does not represent the average users of analytics software. It is like asking your subordinates, who is the best boss.

A good data sample should be random and contain people of different ages and from all walks of life.

You will often see companies misleading consumers with advertising like**:**

"99.99% customer satisfaction rate",

"we are market leaders in …."

All of these claims can be easily validated by looking at the **sample size and sample quality** which they often do not publish for scrutiny.

So it is always good practice to select representative sample which is random and look at the sample size before you draw any conclusions.

You will not get any worthwhile conclusions from bad sample no matter how sophisticated your analysis was.

Takeaways

1. Always look at the sample size before drawing any conclusion.

2. Select random sample from representative population for conducting surveys and data analysis.

Lesson 6: Statistical significance

Statistical significance means statistically meaningful or statistically important.

A statistical significant result is a result which is unlikely to have occurred by chance. Statistically insignificant results are results which are likely to have occurred by chance.

The term 'statistical significance' is used a lot in conversion optimization and especially A/B testing. If the result from your A/B test is not statistically significant than any uplift you see in your A/B test results will not translate into increased sales.

When someone asks you "is your result statistically significant?" then it means he is really asking "What is the likelihood that your result has not occurred by chance".

Consider the following scenario:

	Visits	Transactions	E-Commerce Conversion Rate
Campaign A	1820	150	8.25%
Campaign B	20	4	19.25%
Campaign C	780	41	5.24%

Do you think you should be investing more in campaign B because its conversion rate is highest?

I would suggest, not. The sample size in case of campaign B (4 transactions out of 20 visits) is too small to be statistically significant. Had campaign B got 1 transaction out of 1 visit, it conversion rate would be 100%. Will that make its performance even better? No.

Do you think you should now be investing in campaign A because it has higher conversion rate? Wait a minute. Are you really sure that the difference between the conversion rates of campaign A and campaign C are statistically significant?

In order to determine whether the difference is statistically significant or not, you need to conduct a **statistical test** (for example a Z-test) to calculate the **confidence** that the difference in the conversion rates of the two campaigns is statistically significant.

I am not talking about everyday confidence here, but this **statistical confidence**:

$$\text{confidence} = \frac{\text{signal}}{\text{noise}} \times \sqrt{\text{sample size.}}$$

This is the confidence you need, to play with statistical significance. It is the confidence that the result has not occurred by a random chance.

Statistical significance can be considered to be the confidence one has in a given result.

Confidence depends upon the signal to noise ratio and the sample size.

Noise is the amount of unexplained variation/randomness in a sample.

So confidence that the result has not occurred by a random chance is high if signal is large and/or sample size is large and/or noise is low.

Let us assume that after conducting a statistical test we came to the conclusion that the difference in the conversion rates of the two campaigns cannot be proved to be statistically significant.

Under these circumstances we cannot draw the conclusion that campaign C is not performing better. So what we can do then?

Well we need to collect more data to compute statistical significance of the difference in the conversion rates of the two campaigns. At this stage investing more money in campaign A may not produce optimal results as you may think it will.

As your statistical knowledge grows, you can see yourself conducting more of such statistical tests.

Now back to our campaigns A and C.

In order to find out whether or not the difference in the conversion rates of the two campaigns is statistically significant we need to calculate the confidence i.e. how confident we are statistically, that the difference has not occurred by chance.

If confidence is less than 95% than the difference is not statistically significant and we need to collect more data before drawing any conclusions.

Now let us suppose that the confidence in the difference in the conversion rate of two campaigns, A and C, is 98%:

	E-Commerce Conversion Rate
Campaign A	8.25%
Campaign C	5.24%
Statistical Significance	98%

So what that means is that, we are 98% confident that the difference in conversion rates of the two campaigns, A and B, is not by chance.

Since statistical significance is more than 95%, it means the conversion rate of campaign A is actually higher than the conversion rate of campaign C and is not just an observational error.

Enough theory now, let us see how we can use statistical confidence in real life to take better marketing decisions. Consider the following scenario:

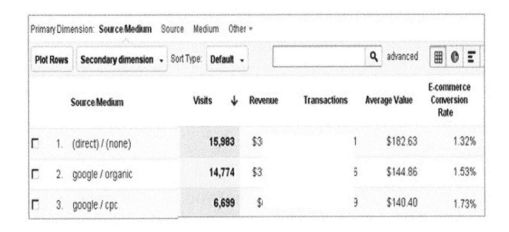

From the table above we can see that the ecommerce conversion rate of Google CPC is higher than that of Google Organic. Does that mean Google CPC campaigns are performing better than organic?

Before we jump to any conclusions and invest more in PPC, let us calculate the statistical significance of the difference in conversion rates of Google organic and PPC campaigns in Google Analytics:

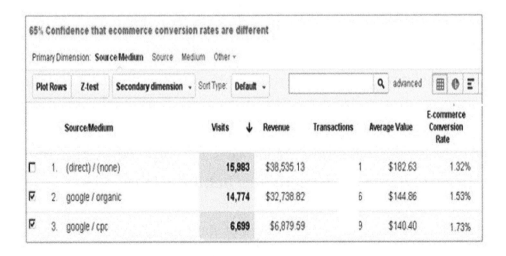

So according to my statistical test (Z-test), I have only 65% confidence that the difference in the conversion rates of Google organic and Google PPC is not by chance.

As confidence is less than 95%, the difference is not statistically significant and we need to collect more data before drawing any conclusions.

To calculate the confidence in my Google analytics report I used the 'Z-test bookmarklet' which you can install from http://www.michaelwhitaker.com/blog/2011/11/02/stats-calculator-google-analytics.

There is one more very important thing that you need to remember.

> *It is possible and quite common for a result to be statistically significant and trivial or statistically insignificant but still important.*

For example, even if the difference in the conversion rates of Google organic and Google PPC turned out to be statistically significant, we should still be investing more in Google organic (in this particular case) as the effect size (in this case revenue) of Google organic is much larger than that of Google PPC.

> *Just because a result is statistically significant, it does not always mean that it is practically meaningful.*

That is why we should interpret both the statistical significance and effect size of our results.

Once you understand what statistical significance is and what statistical significance is not, **you have learned 50% of the statistics behind A/B testing**.

Remember, when someone says to you "this is not statistically significant", he means, it is not statistically meaningful. It is not statistically important.

Now how do statisticians define, what is statistically significant and what is not? They define it through a metric known as **significance level (or confidence level)**

What statistical significance can tell you

Statistical significance only tell you whether or not there is a difference between variation and control.

So when your significance level is 95% or above, you can conclude that there is a difference between control and variation. That's it.

What statistical significance cannot tell you

1. Statistical significance cannot tell you whether variation is better than control. Many marketers wrongly conclude that, just because their test results are statistically significant, their variation is better than control. Remember, statistical significance can only tell you whether or not there is a difference between variation and control.

2. Statistical significance cannot tell you how big or small the difference is between variation and control.

3. Statistical significance cannot tell you whether or not the difference between control and variation is important or helpful in decision making.

4. Statistical significance cannot tell you anything about the magnitude of your test result.

5. Statistical significance cannot tell you whether or not to continue the A/B test.

95% statistical significance does not automatically translate to a 95% chance of beating the original. This is one of the biggest lies every told by creators of A/B testing software.

Lesson 7: Significance level (or confidence level)

Significance level is the value of statistical significance.

Significance level is the level of confidence (denoted by P) in the A/B test result that the difference between control and variation is not by chance.

There are two accepted significance levels:

1. 95%.
2. 99%.

Significance level can also be expressed as the level of confidence in the A/B test result that the difference between control and variation is by chance.

In that case there could be two accepted significance levels:

1. 5%.
2. 1%.

Data scientist rarely use percentages to denote significance level. So significance level of 95% is usually denoted as 0.95 (or 0.05 if the significance level has been expressed in terms of getting results by chance).

Similarly, a significance level of 99% is usually denoted as 0.99 (or 0.01 if the significance level has been expressed in terms of getting results by chance).

For a test result to be statistically important (or statistically significant) the significance level should be 95% or above.

If the significance level is below 95% then a test result is not statistically important.

Two things you need to remember about significance level

1. Significance level changes throughout the duration of A/B test.

So you should never believe in significance level until the test is over.

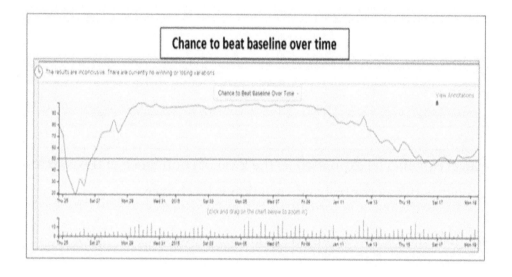

For example, in the first week of running a test, the significance level could be 98%. By the time the second week is over the significance level could drop to 88%. By the time the third week is over the significance level could be 95%. But by the time the fourth week is over significance level could be 60%.

Until your test is over, you cannot trust the significance level. Many marketers stop the test as soon as they see a significance level of 95% or above. This is a big mistake which I will explain further later on.

2. Do not use the significance level to decide whether a test should stop or continue – a significance level of 95% or more means nothing if there is little to no impact on conversion volume.

Lesson 8: Effect and effect size

In statistics 'effect' is the result of something. 'Effect size' (or signal) is the magnitude of a result.

For example, if increasing the daily ad spend of a PPC campaign improves its conversion rate by 2% then 'improvement in conversion rate' is the 'effect' and 'improvement of 2%' is the 'effect size'.

Other examples of effect size are sales, orders, leads, profit etc.

In the case of an A/B test, the effect size (or size of the effect) is the magnitude of your A/B test result.

Effect size is also the magnitude/size of the difference between control and variation. The difference between control and variation is important only when the difference is big.

Formula for calculating the effect size

Effect size
= (mean of experimental group – mean of control group) / standard deviation

If effect size is:

< 0.1 = trivial difference between control and variation.

0.1 – 0.3 = small difference between control and variation.

0.3 – 0.5 = moderate difference between control and variation.

> 0.5 = large difference between control and variation.

Use the effect size value of 0.5 or more, as it indicates a moderate to large difference between control and variation and make the difference meaningful.

You need a large effect size to increase your chances of getting a winning variation, which can actually result in real lift in conversion rate/volume.

> *Statistical significance of 95% or higher does not mean anything, if there is little to no impact on effect size (conversion volume).*

So if you run an ecommerce website then you should **track 'revenue' as a goal for your A/B test.**

By tracking revenue as a goal, you would be able to measure the following metrics in your A/B test results:

1. **Revenue per variation.**

2. **Revenue per product per variation.**

3. **Average revenue per visitor per variation.**

> *Revenue (or sales) is an excellent measure of effect size. It is an excellent measure of the magnitude of A/B test result.*

Similarly, if you run a website which generate leads then you should track the number of leads generated as a goal for your A/B test. The higher the conversion volume (i.e. effect size) per variation the better.

Often marketers set and track trivial goals for their A/B test like CTR, email signups and other micro conversions which is a complete waste of time and resources as they are poor measure of effect size.

> *You have a better chances of getting a real lift in conversions if you track macro conversions as a goal for your A/B test.*

In the case of an A/B test, statistical significance can tell you whether version A is better than version B. But it cannot tell you how good version B is, in a range of contexts.

So what it means is that, if your A/B test reports an uplift of 5% in conversion rate, it does not automatically result in an actual uplift of 5% in conversion rate.

If increasing the conversion rate was so easy, every website owner running A/B tests would be a millionaire by now. So you need to calculate the effect size.

Consider the following campaigns:

	E-Commerce Conversion Rate	Revenue (Effect Size)
Campaign A	8.25%	£600
Campaign C	5.24%	£3,000
Statistical Significance	98%	

From the table above, you can conclude that the effect size (revenue) of campaign C is much higher than the effect size of campaign A.

So even when we are now statistically confident that campaign A has a higher conversion rate than campaign C, we should still be investing more in campaign C because it has much larger effect size.

In the real world, what really matters is the effect size i.e. sales, orders, leads, profits... and not the lame conversion rate.

It is the effect size which puts food on the table. It is the effect size which generates a salary for the employees. It is the effect size which runs business operations.

So whatever you do under conversion optimization must have considerable impact on the effect size. Impact on the conversion rate is secondary.

If you are running A/B tests then it must considerably improve sales and gross profit over time. A double or triple digit increase in conversion rate is meaningless otherwise.

Always take effect size into consideration

Consider the performance of three campaigns A, B and C in the last one month:

	Visits	Transactions	E-Commerce Conversion Rate
Campaign A	1820	150	8.25%
Campaign B	20	4	19.25%
Campaign C	780	41	5.24%

One look at the table above and many marketers will declare campaign B as the winner because it has the highest ecommerce conversion rate. But, as you know by now, this is not the case.

Analysing data without good knowledge of research design and statistics can lead to a serious misinterpretation of data.

Data is not 'what you see is what you get'. Data is 'what you interpret is what you get'.

Here data smart marketers **outsmart** data driven marketers as they tend to look **beyond data**. Since they know data is not 'what you see is what you get', they are less prone to making **observational errors.**

They will go one step further and calculate the effect size (or size of the effect).

If you declare success and failure on the basis of statistical significance alone, then even after conducting several A/B tests and getting statistically significant results each time, there is always a high probability that you will still not see any considerable increase in your revenue.

So if you are making marketing decisions based on statistical significance alone you are not going to get optimal results. You may even, in some cases, loose a significant amount of money.

Therefore it is critical that you always take effect size into consideration while running A/B tests. Optimize your marketing campaigns for effect size (i.e. conversion volume, acquisition cost and gross profit).

Lesson 9: Hypothesis

According to **null hypothesis**, any kind of difference or significance you see in a data set is due to chance and not due to a particular relationship.

For example, according to null hypothesis, any difference in the conversion rates of the two campaigns A and C is due to chance.

To prove that the difference is not due to chance, I need to conduct a statistical test which refutes the null hypothesis.

When null hypothesis is rejected the result is said to be statistically significant.

Important points to remember about null hypothesis

1. Null hypothesis corresponds to a general/default position.

2. Null hypothesis can never be proven.

For example, a statistical test can only reject a null hypothesis or fail to reject a null hypothesis. It cannot prove a null hypothesis.

So if the difference in the conversion rates of the two campaigns A and C is not statistically significant, it does not mean that there is no difference in reality. It only means that there is not enough evidence to reject the null hypothesis that the difference in conversion rates is by chance.

Alternative hypothesis is the opposite of the null hypothesis. According to alternative hypothesis, any kind of difference you see in a data set is due to a particular relationship and not due to chance.

In statistics the only way to prove your hypothesis is to reject the null hypothesis. You do not prove the alternative hypothesis to support your hypothesis.

Before you conduct any test (A/B test, multivariate test or statistical test like T-test or Z-test), you need to form a hypothesis. This hypothesis is based on your understanding of the client's business and quantitative and qualitative data.

For example, null hypothesis can be something like changing the colour of the 'order now' button to red will not improve the conversion rate. So alternative hypothesis will be changing the colour of the 'order now' button to red will improve the conversion rate.

Once you have formed your hypothesis, you conduct a test with the aim to reject your null hypothesis.

An **underpowered hypothesis** is the one which is based on personal opinion or whatever your client/boss has to say. Underpowered hypothesis can also be based on inadequate/flawed analysis or data which has got collection issues. If your hypothesis is underpowered, your A/B test is doomed to fail from the very start.

A **powerful hypothesis** is the one which is based on customer objections and other qualitative and quantitative data.

If you are not already collecting customer objections via surveys, feedback, usability testing, quantitative data etc. then your chances of creating a powerful hypothesis is close to zero. Your chances of getting any real lift from A/B testing is also close to zero.

The power level of your hypothesis is directly proportional to your understanding of the client's business.

The more confident you are, that what you are testing is something that really matters to your customers, the more powerful your hypothesis will become.

You get this confidence by developing a greater understanding of the client's business. You develop this greater understanding by asking questions.

Ask questions which solve your customer's problems either wholly or in part.

This is the fastest way to find and fix conversion issues. Of course you can dive deep into GA reports too.

But, in order to develop a truly great understanding of your client's business you need to ask lot of questions from the people who actually run the business and also their target audience.

Do not try to figure out everything on your own. Any such attempt is not only a waste of time but also futile.

Many marketers make assumption about the problems their customers' are facing. They then create hypothesis around such assumptions and then test and fail spectacularly.

In order to carry out meaningful analysis and create powerful hypothesis, you need to ask questions, lot of questions, tons of questions.

"Every day is a question day.
Every question drives a follow up question."

Ask questions to improve your understanding of the client's business. Ask questions to understand his perspective. Ask questions to quickly deploy solutions. Ask questions to truly embrace agile analytics methodologies.

> *"The art and science of asking questions is the source of all knowledge." - Thomas Berger.*

It took me quite a long time to consciously realize the fact that business questions can never be answered accurately by anyone other than the people who actually run the business.

That no amount of GA reports analysis, Excel hacks, JavaScript, API wrestling or A/B testing can replace the understanding my client has developed over the years by successfully running a profitable business.

That GA reports are the last thing I should be looking at, not the first.

That a knowledge of internet marketing and industry best practice does not automatically make me an expert in any industry I choose to work in.

That I must acknowledge the expertise of my client and come to terms with the fact that my knowledge of his business cannot supersede his understanding of his own business.

That I am here to guide and not to dictate to him how to run his business.

Once I changed my mind-set, I experienced a drastic improvement in my analysis and work life. I no longer needed to live in fear of 'I need to be right' or recommend something which 'has' to work.

I no longer need to spend countless hours going through the GA reports in a hope to find something which may need fixing because I know exactly what needs to be fixed.

I no longer need to chase KPIs because I solve for customers and not for KPIs.

I no longer need to rely just on my own understanding of the client's business to produce recommendations. I no longer need to assume that the problem I am fixing is the one that matters the most to the target audience of my client.

How I am able to do all that? I ask questions, lot of questions, tons of questions.

> *In agile analytics, success does not come from the level of insight you get or the volume of tracking solutions you implement, but from your ability to ask questions which quickly solve your customer problems either wholly or in parts.*

You need to keep asking questions until you reach the underlying source of the problem.

Many people do not ask questions or ask enough questions because of the fear of looking stupid in front of others and/or they just do not want to bother their client/boss every day.

> *"This guy asks a lot of questions. Does he even know what he is doing? He doesn't sound like an expert to me!"*

I used to think like that. Asking too many questions will undermine my professional abilities and make me look clueless. I need to sound like an expert and command like an expert: "Do this or face the consequences".

But that never really worked. I spent countless hours finding a problem which someone, somewhere, in my client's company was already aware of.

What is the point of spending hours and days digging out information/insight which is already known to someone in your organization?

Your time would be best spent finding answers to questions which no one can answer. But for that to happen, you need to know the questions which have already been answered.

You need to overcome your fear of asking questions. I won't lie to you, it is not easy. But you need to find a way to overcome this fear in order to get extraordinary results from your analysis and create a powerful hypothesis.

Ask the question even if your question has already been answered but you either were not paying attention or you did not quite get it.

Ask the question whose answer seems pretty obvious.

Ask even those questions which can be answered just by doing a little research on your own. For example I often ask my clients "where do the majority of your customers live?"

I can easily get an answer to this question by looking at the 'location' report in Google Analytics but I still ask such questions for three main reasons:

1. I am not sure whether the Google Analytics report I am looking at is giving me any accurate insight. Maybe there is some data collection or data sampling issue which is skewing the analytics data.

2. I want to check the understanding of my client about his business. Often such questions disclose a valuable insight. Entrepreneurs who are passionate about their business, usually know a lot about their target market. They often know much more than your GA reports can ever spill out.

3. I want to match the understanding of my client with the insight I am getting from Google Analytics. This way I can quickly detect anomalies in data.

For example, if my client is telling me that their top selling product is 'XYZ' and my GA ecommerce report is telling me that the top selling product is 'PQR' then either my client is wrong or my GA data is wrong. In any case, I now need to do some detective work.

Acknowledge the expertise of your client by asking questions.

We often take our clients for granted when it comes to deciding what is right and what is wrong for their business. They may not know the importance of title tags in search engine ranking. They may not be aware of landing page design best practices. But they do know how to run a business.

Running an online store is not an easy job.

It may look easy but it is not. Try to sell something on eBay or Amazon and you will get my point. Your client is more knowledgeable than you think and you need to acknowledge his expertise, take his input and take advantage of his industry experience in order to fuel your analysis and rapidly deploy solutions.

There is always someone somewhere, standing right under your nose, waiting for you to ask a question and you are looking for the answers in analytics reports. This is not good.

Ask questions every day. You are rewarding your client/boss poorly if you are not asking questions every single day.

Asking questions is a sign of intelligence. It is a sign of understanding. It is a sign of the progress you are making in your analysis. If you do not have any questions to ask then we have got a bigger problem here.

Your client already knows the answer, he is just unaware of it.

If you keep asking questions until you reach the underlying source of the problem, your client will at some point answer his own problem. Trust me on that. It works wonders.

If you are not getting an answer to a problem, you are not asking enough questions.

Raise objections by asking questions. If you think something is not right whether it is pricing, design element, a landing page, campaign budget or targeting then ask 'why'. Ask why it is the way it is?

You will often get useful insight from the client about why things are the way they are. Avoid jumping to conclusions and start making recommendations or start doing testing just because a landing page is not following industry best practices.

The only way to truly benefit from my 'ask questions' strategy is by asking follow up questions. Every question you ask can/should help you in asking more questions so that you can quickly reach the underlying source of the problem.

You need to make asking questions your daily habit. Otherwise you are most likely to forget my tip in a few weeks.

Plan out in advance what questions you will ask tomorrow. Write down somewhere on your work desk that you have to ask questions every day.

The more questions you ask, the better your understanding of the client's business will be and consequently you will be in a better position to create powerful hypothesis.

Once you have created a powerful hypothesis you have won half the battle. The other half can be won by using the knowledge of statistics to design and run your tests.

Lesson 10: False positive and false negative

False positive is a positive test result which is more likely to be false than true.

For example, an A/B test which shows that one variation is better than the other when it is not really the case.

False negative is a negative test result which is more likely to be true than false.

For example, an A/B test which shows that there is no statistical difference between the two variations when there actually is.

Type I error is the incorrect rejection of a true null hypothesis. It represents a false positive error.

Type II error is the failure to reject a false null hypothesis. It represents a false negative error.

All statistical tests have a probability of making type I and type II errors.

The probability of a test to make a type I error is known as **false positive rate** or **significance level** and is denoted by Greek letter alpha α. A significance level of 0.05 means that there is a 5% chance of a false positive.

The probability of a test to make type II error is known as **false negative rate** and is denoted by Greek letter beta β. A false negative rate of 0.05 means that there is a 5% chance of a false negative.

Lesson 11: Statistical power (or power of the A/B test)

Statistical power is the probability of getting statistically significant results.

Statistical power is the probability that your test will accurately find a statistically significant difference between the control and variation when such difference actually exist.

Statistical power is the probability of a statistical test to accurately detect an effect (or accurately rejects the null hypothesis), if the effect actually exists.

It is expressed as a percentage.

> Statistical power (or power of statistical test)
> = 1- false negative rate or 1 - β

So if statistical power of a test is 95% then it means there is 95% probability that the statistical test can correctly detect an effect and 5% probability that it cannot.

This 5% probability that the statistical test cannot correctly detect an effect is the false negative rate.

Lot of A/B test gurus and A/B testing software will tell you to stop your test once you have reached a statistical significance of 95% or more.

Now the problem with this approach is that, you will continue testing until you get a statistically significant result, while choosing the sample size as you go with your test.

The consequence of this approach is that your probability of getting a statistically significant result by coincidence will go much higher than 5%.

That means you will increase your chance of getting type I error in your test. That means your test will increase the rate of false positives.

The fundamental problem with statistics is that, if you want to reach to the conclusion you really want (may be deep down inside on a subconscious level), you can always find some way to do it.

> *To reduce the rate of false positives, decide your test sample size in advance and then just stick to it.*

Do not use statistical significance alone to decide whether your test should continue or stop. Statistical significance of 95% or higher does not mean anything, if there is little to no impact on effect size (conversion volume).

Do not believe in any uplift you see in your A/B test until the test is over. Focus on the effect size per variation while the test is running.

Any uplift you see in you A/B test results will not translate into actual sales even after conducting several A/B tests and getting statistically significant results each time, if:

1. There is little to no impact on effect size (conversion volume).
2. You declare success and failure on the basis of statistical significance alone.

It is widely accepted that statistical power should be 80% (0.8) or greater. If the statistical power is less than 0.8 then you need to increase your sample size.

Why is statistical power important? This is because marketers who do not understand statistical power generally end up running underpowered A/B test.

Underpowered A/B tests

An underpowered test is the one which has got inadequate sample size.

Avoid running underpowered A/B tests.

Underpowered A/B tests greatly increase the likelihood of getting false positive or false negative results.

Statistical power is related to sample size and minimum detectable effect.

Statistical power increases with sample size as a large sample means you have collected more information.

If you take a very small sample size for your A/B test then the statistical power of the test will be very small. In other words, the probability that your A/B test will accurately find a statistically significant difference between the control and variation is going to be very small.

If you take a big sample size for your A/B test then the statistical power of the test will be big. In other words, the probability that your A/B test will accurately find a statistically significant difference between the control and variation is going to be high.

Overpowered A/B tests

An overpowered A/B test is the one which has got much more than sufficient sample size.

Avoid running overpowered A/B tests.

When the statistical power of your A/B test is 80%, there is a 20% probability of making type II error (or false negative error).

When you run an overpowered A/B test, the statistical power of A/B test becomes greater than 80% which decreases the probability of getting type II errors but at the same time increases the probability of getting type I error (or false positive error).

Statisticians worldwide consider a type I error to be four times more serious than a type II error because finding something that is not there is considered a more serious error than the failure to find something that is there.

That's why the statistical power of your A/B test should not exceed or go below 80% (or 0.8).

Not only do overpowered A/B tests increase your chances of getting false positive results but they also waste your time and resources by collecting more test data than needed.

Lesson 12: Minimum detectable effect

Minimum detectable effect (MDE) is the smallest amount of change that you want to detect from the baseline/control.

For example:

1% MDE = detect changes in conversion rate of 1% or more. You will not be able to detect changes in conversion rate which is less than 1%.

10% MDE = detect changes in conversion rate of 10% or more. You will not be able to detect changes in conversion rate which is less than 10%.

40% MDE = detect changes in conversion rate of 40% or more. You will not be able to detect changes in conversion rate which is less than 40%.

There is a strong correlation between minimum detectable effect and sample size

The smaller your MDE, the larger the sample size you will need per variation. Conversely, the bigger your MDE, the smaller the sample size you will need per variation. This is because you need less traffic to detect big changes and more traffic to detect small changes. That is why it is prudent to **make and test big changes.**

Lesson 13: Outliers

An outlier is an extreme value in a data set.

You need to keep your A/B test results free from outliers

If you are tracking any goal which is an average metric (such as average revenue per visitor) than the presence of outliers (extremely large values), for example a few abnormally large orders, can easily skew the test results.

The solution to this problem is to stop any abnormally large value from passing to your A/B test results in the first place.

So if you are tracking revenue as a goal in your A/B testing tool, you should set up a code which filters out abnormally large orders from your test results.

For example, if your website's average order value in the last three months has been $150 then any order which is above $200 can be considered as an outlier.

You can write some code which does not allow any purchase order greater than $200 to pass to your A/B testing tool. Refer to the documentation of your A/B testing tool for more details.

Lesson 14: Confidence interval

Confidence interval is the amount of error allowed in A/B testing. It is the measure of the reliability of an estimate.

It can be expressed as 20.0% ± 2.0%.

Confidence interval is made up of conversion rate and margin of error.

For example:

A confidence interval for control of 15% ± 2% means it is likely that 13% to 17% of the visitors to the control version of the web page may convert. Here 15% is the conversion rate of the control version of the web page and **± 2%** is the margin of error.

A confidence interval for variation of 30% ± 3% means it is likely that 27% to 33% of the visitors to the variation page may convert. Here 30% is the conversion rate of the variation page and ± 3% is the margin of error.

There should not be any overlap of confidence intervals between control and variation, as it means that you need a bigger sample size and to continue the test.

For example, if a confidence interval of original is 37.10% ± 8.54 and confidence interval of variation is 50.00% ± 8.56 then there is an overlapping of confidence interval and hence you need a bigger sample size and you need to continue the test:

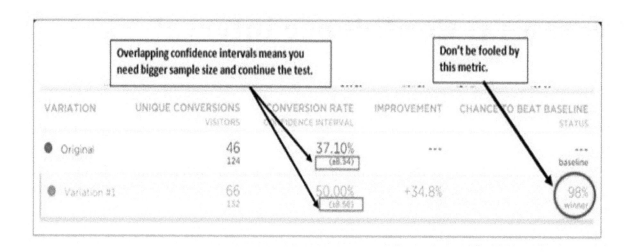

Overlapping confidence intervals means you
need bigger sample size and continue the test.

Don't be fooled by
this metric.

VARIATION	UNIQUE CONVERSIONS	CONVERSION RATE	IMPROVEMENT	CHANCE TO BEAT BASELINE
	VISITORS	CONFIDENCE INTERVAL		STATUS
● Original	46 / 124	37.10% (±8.34)	· · ·	· · · / baseline
● Variation #1	66 / 132	50.00% (±8.56)	+34.8%	98% winner

290

Lesson 15: Conversion rate and improvement metrics in A/B testing

In the context of A/B testing:

> *Conversion rate is the percentage of unique visitors who saw the control or variation page and then completed a goal.*

It is a calculated as:

> *Conversion rate*
> *= conversions / unique visitors who saw the control or variation page*

Another metric which is widely reported by A/B testing software is '**improvement**'.

In the context of A/B testing:

> *Improvement is the relative difference between conversion rate of variation and conversion rate of control.*

For example:

If 30% is the conversion rate of the variation page and 15% is the conversion rate of the control version of the web page then

Improvement = 30% − 15%
= 15 percentage points or 100% ([30-15] / 15 * 100)

So an improvement of 100% means there is a 100% increase in conversion rate for the variation page. Although such improvements generally do not translate into an actual lift in conversion.

Lesson 16: Confounding variables

Confounding variables are those variables which a tester failed to identify / control / eliminate/ measure while conducting an A/B test.

Confounding variables (also known as third variables or confounding factors) can adversely affect the relationship between dependant and independent variables thus leading to a false positive results.

Presence of confounding variables is a sign of weakness in the experiment design.

You must identify as many confounding variables as possible before starting an A/B test and then eliminate or minimize their adverse effects on your test.

The following confounding factors, if they occur in the middle of an A/B test, can considerably impact your website traffic and hence skew the test results:

1. New marketing campaigns launched.

2. Certain marketing campaigns turned off.

3. Occurrence of special events like Christmas, New Year or any public holiday.

4. Major positive or negative news/announcement about your website/ business like:

    a) New product launch.

b) New business division launch.

c) Closure of a business division.

d) Departure/appointment of a key employee/executive.

e) Media mention etc.

5. Major update to search engine algorithm.

6. Complete redesign of the website.

7. Redesign of the control and/or variation pages.

8. Website hit with a new search engine penalty or got rid of an existing penalty.

9. Prolonged website outage or some other server side issue.

10. Major website crawling and/or indexing issues (like unwanted robots.txt exclusion which negatively impact the organic search traffic and direct traffic).

11. Change in experiment settings.

12. Change in test goals.

Avoid changing experiment settings in the middle of a test. For example, if you changed the amount of traffic allocated to original, and each variation in the middle of the test then it can easily skew your test results as one variation could end up getting lot more returning visitors than the others.

This skews the test results as returning visitors have got a higher probability of making a purchase.

If you think it is absolutely necessary to change the traffic allocation settings in the middle of a test then by all means do it. But then reset the test and restart it.

Similarly, do not change your test goals in the middle of a test as it can skew your test results. However if you think it is absolutely necessary to change the goals then do it. But then rest the test and restart it.

> *Make notes of confounding factors that affect your test by creating annotation on the test results' chart.*

The majority of A/B tests fail simply because of the presence of confounding variables which skew the test results.

Lesson 17: The multiple comparisons problem

Avoid running A/B/C/D tests!

The more test variations you create and compare with the control, the higher the probability of getting false positive results. This issue is commonly known as **the multiple comparisons problem.**

The other disadvantage of testing multiple variations is that, the more variations you have in your test, the more traffic you would need to get test results which are statistically significant and thus longer it will take to finish the test.

So keep your test variants to a minimum. That means avoid A/B/C tests or A/B/C/D tests or A/B/C/D/E tests!

Lesson 18: Predictive analytics

Predictive analytics is an area of statistical analysis in which we extract information from data and then analyse it to identify patterns and make predictions about future outcomes/events.

Both trend analysis and regression analysis are subsets of predictive analysis.

In trend analysis we extract information from data and then analyse the information to identify patterns in that information.

In regression analysis we make predictions about future outcomes/events by estimating the relationship between two or more variables.

Regression analysis is based on the idea that what has happened in the past can give us an idea of what can happen in the future.

Predictive analytics can be applied to a wide range of industries like sports, real estate, insurance, marketing etc.

Predictive marketing

Predictive marketing is the application of predictive analytics in marketing.

Predictive marketing can help you answer the following questions:

- What are my sales likely to be for the second half of the year?
- Where should I invest my money and resources to get the highest possible ROI?

- Where will current business operations and marketing practices take me?
- Which customers are most likely to respond to our new social media campaign?

...the questions are endless.

Predictive marketing is difficult to learn and equally difficult to implement. I want to be honest with you, there is a steep learning curve.

In order to learn predictive marketing techniques you need to climb a pyramid in which each step is progressively more difficult than the last:

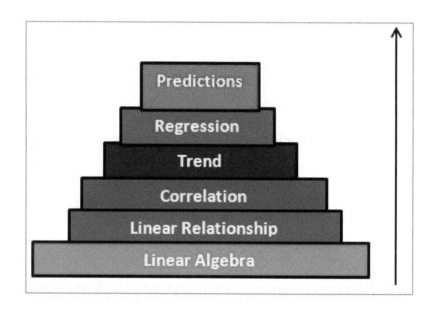

But once you have climbed all the steps and reached the top, you can make predictions which are statistically accurate.

In order to learn predictive marketing you need to first know or learn 'linear algebra', followed by 'linear relationship', 'correlation', 'trends' and 'regression'.

Only once you know all these concepts can you proceed to making predictions in a scientific way.

Linear algebra

Slope (gradient) of a straight line

The slope of a straight line defines how steep the line is.

> *Slope*
>
> *= change in vertical distance /change in horizontal distance*

Note: The change in height is also called 'rise' or 'fall'. Change in horizontal distance is also called 'run'.

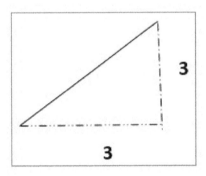

The slope of this line

=3/3

=1

Note: Large slope means steeper line. For example:

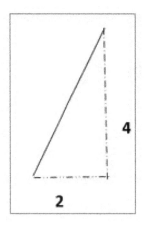

Here the slope of line

= 4/2

= 2

A slope can be positive, negative, zero or undefined.

Positive slope – A slope is positive if both change in horizontal distance and vertical distance is positive. For example:

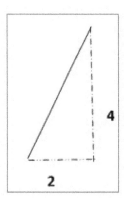

Here the slope of line

= 4/2

= 2

Negative slope – A slope is negative if change in horizontal distance is negative or change in vertical distance is negative. For example:

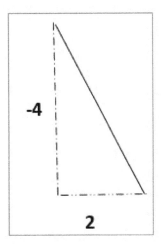

Here the slope of the line

= -4/2

= -2

Zero slope - A slope is zero if change in vertical distance is zero. For example:

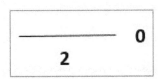

Here the slope of the line

= 0/2

= 0

Undefined slope – A slope is undefined if the change in horizontal distance is zero. For example:

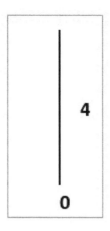

Here the slope of the line

= 4/0

= undefined

Y intercept of a straight line

The Y intercept of a straight line is the point where a line crosses the y-axis. For example:

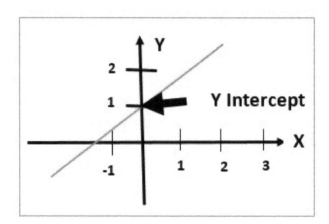

In the diagram the line crosses the y-axis at 1. So here the y intercept is 1.

Equation of a straight line

The equation of a straight line is:

$Y = mX + b$

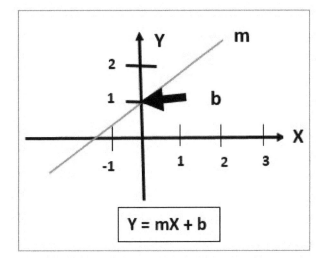

Y = mX + b

Here m is the slope of the straight line and b is the y intercept.

For example let us calculate the equation of the following straight line:

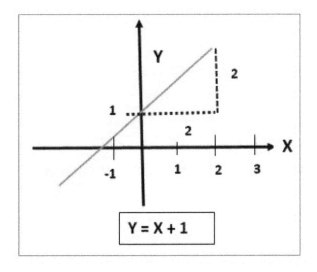

Y = X + 1

Here the slope

= 2/2

= 1

So m = 1

The Y intercept = 1

So b = 1

So the equation of the straight line is y = x + 1

Linear relationship

If a linear relationship exists between two variables then an increase or decrease in the value of one variable will cause a corresponding increase or decrease in the value of the other variable.

This type of relationship exists between **dependent and independent variables**.

For example, suppose you want to forecast the sales for your company and you have concluded that your sales go up and down depending on changes in average order value (AOV).

The sales you are forecasting would be the dependent variable because its value **depends** on the value of AOV, and the AOV would be the independent variable.

An independent variable is generally denoted by the letter 'x'. Whereas a dependant variable is generally denoted by the letter 'y'.

In a cause and effect relationship, the independent variable is the cause and the dependent variable is the effect.

You can express a linear relationship between 'x' and 'y' via the equation of the straight line: y=mx+b

Here 'm' is the slope of the straight line and 'b' is the y-intercept. You can also express a linear relationship in a graphical format via an Excel scatter chart like this:

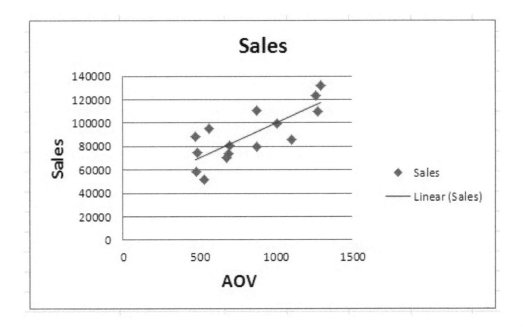

Note: In regression analysis we predict the value of a dependent variable from one or more independent variables.

How can you determine whether the relationship between two variables is linear or not?

There are two methods to determine a linear relationship between two variables:

1. Through an Excel scatter chart.
2. Through a residual plot.

Excel scatter chart

Step 1: To determine how two variables are related, graph the data points using an Excel scatter chart so that the independent variable is on the x axis and the dependent variable is on the y-axis.

In your Excel table, make sure that the column of data that you want to display on the x-axis is located to the left of the column of data you want to display on the y-axis. Something like this:

E	F
X (indepedant)	Y (dependant)
1260	123118
1007	99601
1296	132000
873	80000
532	52000
476	58625
482	74624
1273	110000
692	81000
690	73507
564	95024
470	88004
675	70000
870	110253
1100	86000

Step 2: Once you have plotted the data points. You will see a graph something like the one below:

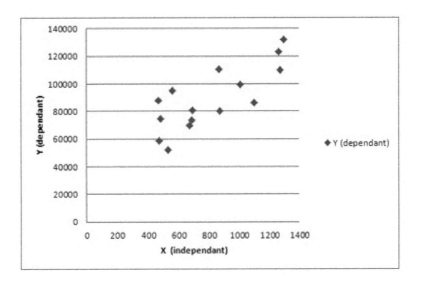

If you look at the data points, you can see that they resemble a straight line:

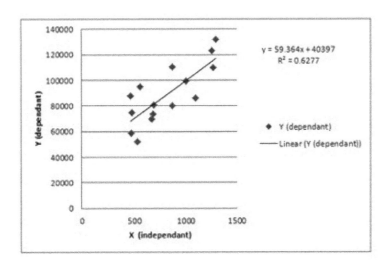

Here I have added a trend line to make this look more obvious.

Trend lines are used to graphically display trends in data.

To add a trend line to your chart, follow the steps below in MS Excel 2013:

1. Select the chart and then click on the design tab in the Excel ribbon.

2. Click on the 'add chart element' button and then select 'trend line', then 'linear'

Note: A trend line is also known as a 'regression line' or a 'least square line'

Residual plot

A residual (denoted by e) is the difference between the observed value and the predicted value of a dependant variable in regression analysis. Each data point has one residual.

> *Residual (e)*
> *= observed value – predicted value*

For example:

=F4-G4

D	E	F	G	H
	X (indepedant)	Y (dependant)	Predicted Cost	Errors (Residuals)
	1260	123118	115195.4579	7922.5421
	1007	99601	100176.4165	-575.4165
	1296	132000	117332.5547	14667.4453
	873	80000	92221.6673	-12221.6673
	532	52000	71978.6115	-19978.6115
	476	58625	68654.2387	-10029.2387
	482	74624	69010.4215	5613.5785
	1273	110000	115967.1873	-5967.1873
	692	81000	81476.8195	-476.8195
	690	73507	81358.0919	-7851.0919
	564	95024	73878.2531	21145.7469
	470	88004	68298.0559	19705.9441
	675	70000	80467.6349	-10467.6349
	870	110253	92043.5759	18209.4241
	1100	86000	105697.2499	-19697.2499

Note: Residuals are also called as **errors** or **regression residuals**.

In the table above column F contains all the observed values of the dependant variable y.

The column G contains all the predicted values of the dependant variable y.

The column H contains the residuals.

Note: Both the sum and the mean of the residuals is equal to zero.

A residual plot is a graph that shows all the residuals on the vertical axis and the independent variable on the horizontal axis.

If the points in a residual plot are randomly dispersed around the horizontal axis then the relationship between two variables is linear otherwise it is non-linear.

For example, the following residual plot shows a linear relationship as the data points are randomly dispersed around the horizontal axis:

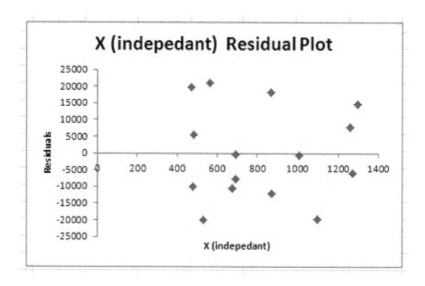

Now look at the following residual plots:

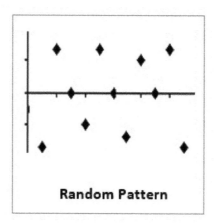

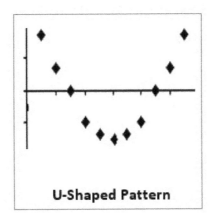

U-Shaped Pattern

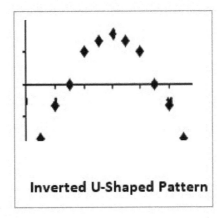

Inverted U-Shaped Pattern

Here the first residual plot shows a linear relationship. The other two plots show a non-linear relationship as the data points are not randomly dispersed around the horizontal axis.

Note 1: The sum of the residuals is always zero, whether the data set is linear or non-linear.

Note 2: You need to conduct regression analysis in order to create residual plots. I will teach you later how to create a residual plot.

Correlation

A correlation is a statistical measurement of a relationship between two variables.

A correlation measures how two variables change in relation to each other.

The formula used to calculate the relationship between two variables is called **covariance**:

$$Cov(x, y) = \sum \frac{(x_n - x_u)(y_n - y_u)}{N}$$

Covariance measures the **strength and direction of the relationship** between two variables. It is a measure of how much two variables change together.

Let us suppose x and y are two variables. If as x goes up, y goes up then covariance would be positive. However if as x goes up, y goes down then covariance would be negative.

The problem with calculating covariance is that the number you get from the calculation is hard to interpret. This happens because covariance in not normalized (statistically adjusted).

Correlation coefficient is the normalized version of covariance and is calculated as:

Correlation coefficient
= covariance / product of the standard deviation of the two variables.

Note: Correlation coefficient is not useful if the relationship between variables is non-linear.

The most common correlation coefficient is **'Pearson product-moment correlation coefficient'** which measures the strength and direction of the linear relationship (relationship which resembles a straight line) between variables.

When we speak simply of a correlation coefficient, we are generally referring to the 'Pearson product-moment correlation'.

'Spearman's rank correlation' and 'Kendall rank correlation' are also types of correlations.

The **correlation coefficient of a sample** (sample is set of observations drawn from a population) is denoted by r.

The **correlation coefficient of a population** (population is total set of observations) is denoted by R or ρ.

The value of correlation coefficient can range from +1 to -1. The sign (positive or negative) of the correlation coefficient describes the direction of the relationship between two variables.

The absolute value of the correlation coefficient describes the strength of the relationship between two variables.

Correlation of +1 means that the variables x and y have strongest positive linear relationship i.e. when x is larger than average, y tends to be larger than average. Similarly when x is smaller than average, y tends to be smaller than average.

Correlation of -1 means that the variables x and y have strongest negative linear relationship i.e. when x is larger than average, y tends to be smaller than average. Similarly when x is smaller than average, y tends to be larger than average.

Correlation of 0 means that no linear relationship exist between the two variables. Keep in mind that the 'Pearson product-moment correlation coefficient' only measures linear relationships.

Therefore, a correlation coefficient of 0 does not mean a zero relationship exists between two variables. It simply means no linear relationship exists between the two variables. It is possible for two variables to have a **curvilinear relationship** (it is a non-linear relationship which does not resemble a straight line) instead of a linear relationship.

A correlation greater than 0.8 is generally considered as a strong correlation, whereas a correlation less than 0.5 is generally considered as a weak correlation.

However, these values can vary based upon the type of data being analysed.

Now consider the following scatter charts:

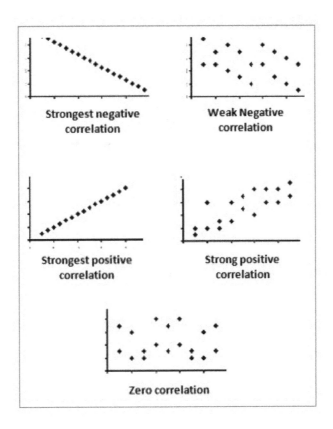

We can conclude the following facts from the above scatter charts:

1. In the case of a positive correlation the slope of the straight line is positive. Whereas in the case of a negative correlation the slope of the straight line is negative.

2. In the case of a **strongest positive correlation (r=1) or strongest negative correlation (r=-1)** the data points form an exact straight line.

3. The correlation becomes weaker as the data points become more scattered. So in the case of a zero correlation the data points are completely scattered (in a random manner).

Outliers effect correlation

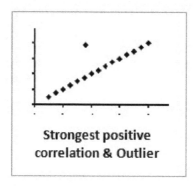

Strongest positive
correlation & Outlier

Outliers are extreme values that differ greatly from other values.

In regression analysis the data points that diverge greatly from the overall pattern of the data are called outliers.

Note: If the values of the two variables are unreliable (because of measurement error or other errors) then the correlation coefficient could be lower than expected.

Correlation coefficient and predictive power

A correlation coefficient (R) is a good indicator of a predictive relationship between two variables. For example:

If the value of R is zero then the dependent variable cannot be predicted from the independent variable as the relationship between two variables is nonlinear.

If the value of R is 1 or -1 then the dependent variable can be predicted without any error from the independent variable.

If the value of R between 0 and 1 or 0 or -1 measures the extent to which the dependant variable is predictable from the independent variable.

For example an R of 0.50 means that 50% of the variation in the dependant variable (y) is predictable from the independent variable (x). The other 50% variation in y cannot be explained.

Similarly an R of 0.20 means that 20% of the variation in the dependant variable (y) is predictable from the independent variable (x). The other 80% variation in y cannot be explained.

Therefore it is important that you determine the correlation between two variables before you run regression analysis.

If there is no linear relationship or a weak linear relationship between two variables, or in other words the correlation between the two variables is zero or weak, then such a relationship is not good for predicting anything so there is no point running a regression analysis.

Coefficient of determination or R-squared value

1st definition – The coefficient of determination (denoted by R^2 or R-squared value) is a number from 0 to 1 that describes how well a regression line (i.e. trend line) fits a data set. A trend line is most reliable/accurate when its R^2 value is 1 or near 1.

2nd definition – The coefficient of determination (denoted by R^2) is a number from 0 to 1 that measures the percentage of variation in the dependent variable that is predictable from the independent variable(s).

3rd definition - The coefficient of determination (denoted by R^2) is the square of the correlation coefficient (R).

4th definition – The coefficient of determination allows to interpret the relationship between two variables in terms of variation.

5th definition - The coefficient of determination is the ratio of 'explained variation' to the total variation.

If the value of R2 is 0 then the dependent variable cannot be predicted from the independent variable.

If the value of R2 is 1 then the dependent variable can be predicted without any error from the independent variable.

The value of R2 between 0 and 1 measures the extent to which the dependant variable is predictable from the independent variable.

For example, an R2 of 0.50 means that 50% of the variation in the dependant variable (y) is predictable from the independent variable (x). The other 50% variation in y cannot be explained.

Similarly, an R2 of 0.20 means that 20% of the variation in the dependant variable (y) is predictable from the independent variable (x). The other 80% variation in y cannot be explained.

For example, in the chart below 62% of the variation in sales can be explained by the variation in AOV. The remaining 38% (100-62) variation in sales can be explained by other factors.

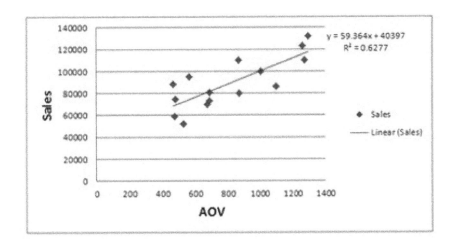

The other factors that can explain the variation in sales can be determined by running multiple regression analysis.

Note: Coefficient of determination is a key output of regression analysis.

How to display the R-squared value on your chart

To display this value on your chart, follow the steps below:

Step 1: In MS Excel 2013, right click on the trend line and then select 'format trend line' from the drop down menu. This will open up the 'format trend line' box on the right hand side of the Excel window.

Step 2: In the 'format trend line' box, select the checkbox 'display R-squared value on chart':

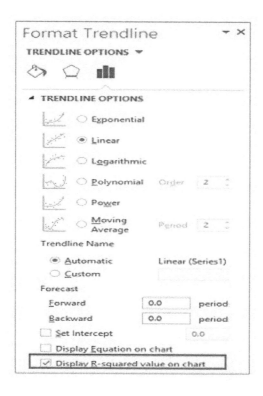

You can now see the R-squared value in your chart like the one below:

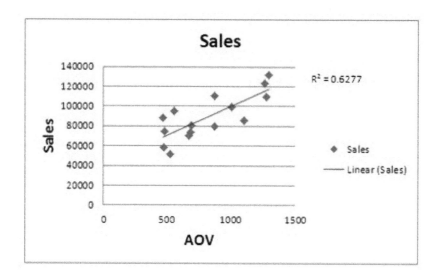

Note: When you add a trend line to a chart, Excel automatically calculates the R-squared value of the trend line.

Methods to find a correlation between two sets of data

There are three methods of finding a correlation between two sets of data in Excel:

1. Using the Analysis ToolPak.
2. Using the CORREL function.
3. Using the R2 Value.

Using the Analysis ToolPak for finding a correlation between two data sets

The Analysis ToolPak is an Excel add-in through which you can do complex statistical analysis (like multiple regressions) in Excel.

It is available in Excel 2007 and above versions. To install Analysis ToolPak in Excel 2013, follow the steps below:

Step 1: Open MS Excel and then click on the file tab.

Step 2: Go to options, then Excel options, then add-ins.

Step 3: Select the Analysis ToolPak option and then click on the 'go' button.

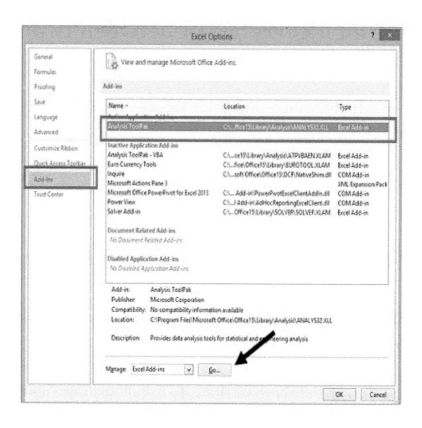

Step 4: Select the Analysis ToolPak check box and then click on the 'ok' button:

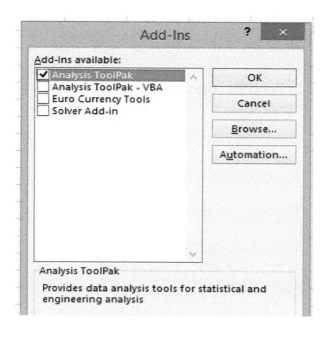

Once the Analysis ToolPak is installed, you would see the new 'data analysis' button on the extreme right under the data tab:

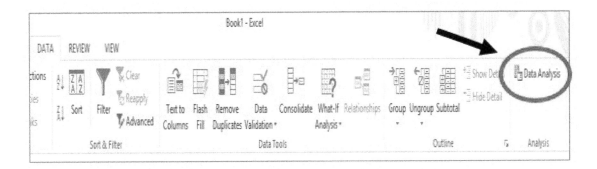

Now click on the 'data analysis' button, select 'correlation' from the list and then click on the 'ok' button:

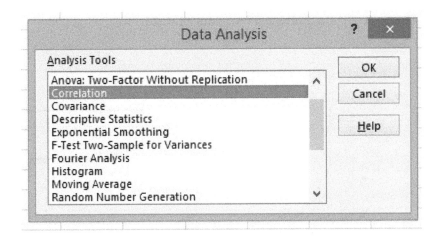

Select the 'input range' (the two columns in this case) and output range (where you want to display the results) and then click on the ok button:

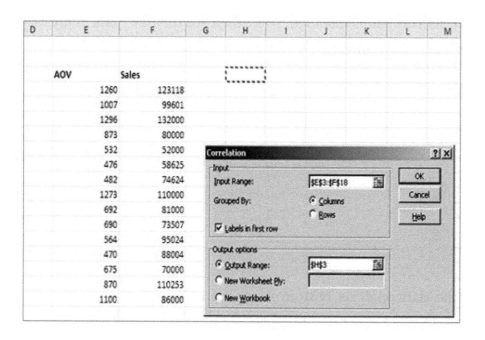

You can now see the correlation between two sets of data:

E	F	G	H	I	J
AOV	**Sales**			*AOV*	*Sales*
1260	123118		AOV	1	
1007	99601		Sales	0.792282	1
1296	132000				
873	80000				
532	52000				
476	58625				
482	74624				
1273	110000				
692	81000				
690	73507				
564	95024				
470	88004				
675	70000				
870	110253				
1100	86000				

Here the correlation between AOV and sales is 0.792282.

Using the CORREL function for finding a correlation between two data sets

Through this Excel function you can calculate the correlation between two data sets without using the Analysis ToolPak.

   Syntax: CORREL (array1, array2)

For example:

D	E	F	G	H	I	J
	AOV	Sales			AOV	Sales
		1260	123118	AOV		1	
		1007	99601	Sales	0.792282	1
		1296	132000			
		873	80000		0.792282266	
		532	52000			
		476	58625			
		482	74624			
		1273	110000			
		692	81000			
		690	73507			
		564	95024			
		470	88004			
		675	70000			
		870	110253			
		1100	86000			

fx =CORREL(E4:E18,F4:F18)

Here the correlation between AOV and Sales is 0.792282.

This is the same value we got when we used the Analysis ToolPak to calculate the correlation between two data sets.

Using the R2 value for finding a correlation between two data sets

The correlation between two data sets can also be defined as the square root of the R2 value:

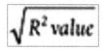

$$\sqrt{R^2\ value}$$

You can calculate the R2 value by using the RSQ Excel function.

Syntax: RSQ (known_y's, known_x's)

Here known_y's are the values of dependent variable (in this case sales) and known_x's are the values of independent variable (in this case AOV (average order value)).

For example:

f_x	=RSQ(F4:F18,E4:E18)						
D	E	F	G	H	I	J
	AOV	Sales			AOV	Sales
	1260	123118		AOV	1	
	1007	99601		Sales	0.792282	1
	1296	132000				
	873	80000		0.792282266		
	532	52000		R2 Value	0.627711	
	476	58625				
	482	74624				
	1273	110000				
	692	81000				
	690	73507				
	564	95024				
	470	88004				
	675	70000				
	870	110253				
	1100	86000				

Once you have determined the R2 value then take its square root via the Excel function SQRT to determine the correlation between two data sets.

For example:

fx	=SQRT(I8)						
D	E	F	G	H	I	J	
	AOV	Sales				AOV	Sales
	1260	123118		AOV		1	
	1007	99601		Sales		0.792282	1
	1296	132000					
	873	80000			0.792282266		
	532	52000		R2 Value		0.627711	
				Correlation by			
				using			
	476	58625		R2 Value		0.792282	
	482	74624					
	1273	110000					
	692	81000					
	690	73507					
	564	95024					
	470	88004					
	675	70000					
	870	110253					
	1100	86000					

Note: The correlation determined through R2 value matches the correlation determined through CORREL function and the correlation determined through Analysis ToolPak.

Trend analysis basics

A trend is a movement in a particular direction.

We do trend analysis for the following reasons:

1. To measure the performance of a marketing campaign over a period of time. Through trend analysis you can identify areas where your campaign is performing well (so that you can replicate success) and the areas where your campaign is underperforming.

2. Trend analysis helps in getting answers to questions like:

    a. What are my top selling products?
    b. What are my top converting keywords?
    c. Which keywords should I bid on?
    d. Where should I invest my money and resources to get the highest possible ROI?
    e. Which are the most effective marketing channels in terms of conversions and revenue?

3. Trend analysis helps in determining where current business operations and marketing practices could take you. Negative trends act as a warning of potential problems with current practices.

4. Trend analysis can help in refining business decisions and strategies. We develop strategies which respond to the identified trends. Moving with positive trends and not against them can lead to more profit.

5. Trend analysis can help in identifying risks and opportunities.

6. Through trend analysis we can predict future outcomes and events such as what the sales for the second half of the year are likely to be.

The importance of accurately analysing and interpreting data trends

How we analyse and interpret the data trends plays a very important role in optimizing our marketing campaigns and making predictions about future outcomes.

One wrong interpretation and we can end up losing hundreds of thousands of dollars (depending upon the size of your business).

Important points to keep in mind while analysing, interpreting and reporting data trends

1. Always question how the data is collected.

2. Understand that historical data is in fact 'dated'.

3. Select the right time period to analyse your data trends.

4. Add comparison to your data trends.

5. Never report standalone metric in your data trends.

6. Segment your data before you analyse/report data trends.

7. Report something business bottom-line impacting.

8. Make the insight obvious.

9. Use sparklines and conditional formatting.

10. Do not jump to conclusions.

11. Analysing a single trend is rarely useful.

Types of trend

1. **Uptrend** – moving higher.

2. **Downtrend** – moving lower.

3. **Sideways / horizontal trend** – moving sideways.

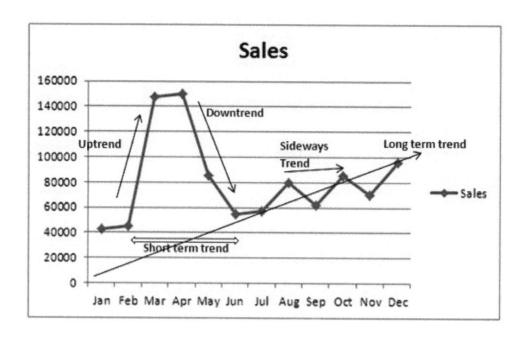

Note: A sideways trend is technically not a trend. It is the lack of a well-defined trend in either direction.

Trend length

A trend can be short (or seasonal), intermediate or long term. The longer the trend the more significant it is.

For example, a three month trend is not as significant as a three year trend.

Regression analysis

Regression analysis is a statistical technique which is used to estimate a relationship between a dependant variable and one or more independent variables.

In regression analysis we try to predict the value of a dependant variable (y) from one or more independent variables (x1, x2, x3 etc.)

*When we use one independent variable to predict the value of a dependent variable then this type of regression is known as **linear regression**.*

The analysis which is done in linear regression is known as **linear regression analysis**.

*When we use two or more independent variables to predict the value of a dependent variable then this type of regression is known as **multiple regression**.*

The analysis which is done in multiple regression is known as **multiple regression analysis**.

The equation used to calculate linear regression is
$$y = a + bX$$

Here y is the dependant variable (the variable whose value we are trying to predict).

X is the independent variable (the variable whose value we are using to predict the value of y).

a is the y-intercept.

b is the slope of the regression line.

The equation used to calculate multiple regression is
$$Y = a + b_1X_1 + b_2X_2 + b_3X_3 + \dots b_nX_n$$

Here y is the dependant variable (the variable whose value we are trying to predict).

X_1, X_2, X_3, X_n are the independent variables (the variables whose values we are using to predict the value of y).

a is the 'y-intercept'.

b1, b2, b3, bn are the slope of the regression lines.

Note: You can use up to 15 independent variables in Excel to do multiple regression analysis.

By doing regression analysis, you can extend a trend line in a chart beyond the actual data in order to predict the future values of the dependant variable.

For example, the following chart uses a trend line that is forecasting four months ahead and is clearly showing a trend of an increase in sales.

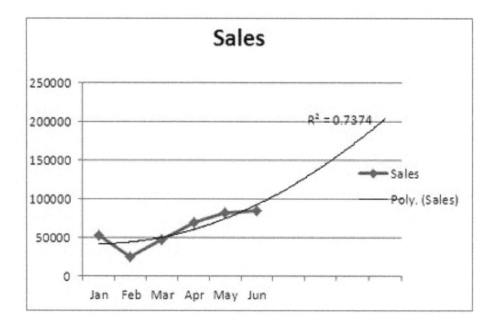

However for regression analysis to work you need to select the right trend line for your data in the first place.

Choosing the best trend line for your data

Choosing the right trend line for your data is very important. If you apply the wrong trend line then your predictions/forecasts will not be accurate.

The R2 value can help you in choosing the best trend line for your data.

There are six types of trend lines (or regression lines) available in Excel:

1. Linear trend line.

2. Logarithmic trend line.

3. Polynomial trend line.

4. Moving average trend line.

5. Power trend line.

6. Exponential trend line.

Add each of the trend line in turns and note down its R2 value. The trend line whose R2 value is highest is the best trend line to use.

Linear trend line

Use this trend line if your data set is linear (resembles a straight line) and the data values are increasing or decreasing at a steady rate.

For example, the following chart contains a linear trend line as visits are increasing at a steady rate:

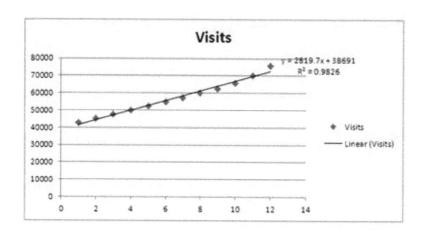

To add a linear trend line to your chart follow the steps below:

Step 1: Right click on the data points in your chart and then select the 'add trend line' option:

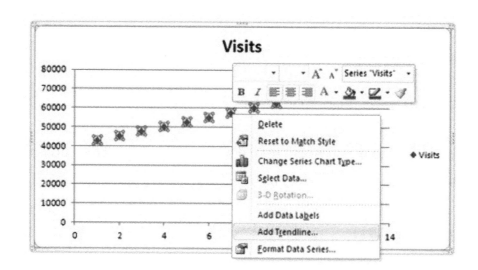

Step 2: From the 'format trend line' dialog box select 'linear' and select the two check boxes called 'display equation on chart' and 'display R-squared value on chart':

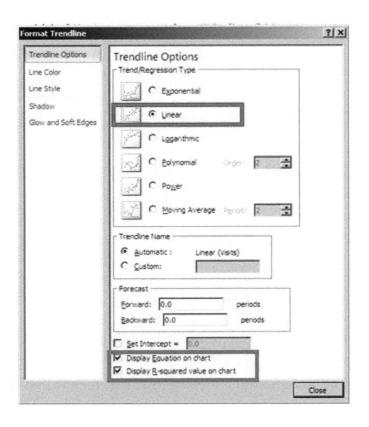

Step 3: Click on the 'close' button. You will now see the updated chart with the linear trend line, linear trend line equation and R2 value:

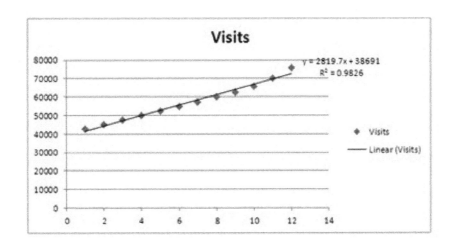

Use the same procedure to add other type of trend lines to your chart.

The equation used to calculate the linear trend line is:

$$Y = mx + b$$

Here y is the dependant variable, m is the slope of the line and b is the y intercept.

Excel automatically calculates the linear trend line for you once you applied it to your chart.

In the chart above the equation used to display the linear trend line is:

$$y = 2819.7x + 38691$$

Here 2189.7 is the slope of the line and 38691 is the y-intercept.

Also note the R2 value of 0.9826, which is close to 1. This means that this trend line is very reliable.

Logarithmic trend line

Use this trend line if your data values increases or decreases quickly and then levels out.

For example, the following chart contains a logarithmic trend line as visits increases quickly and then levels out:

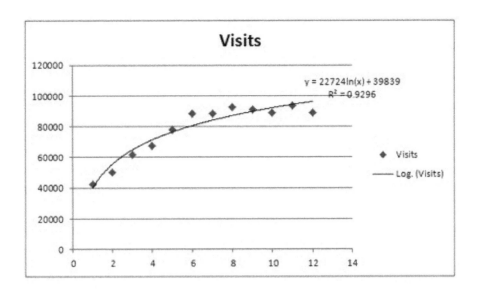

The equation used to calculate the logarithmic trend line is:

$y = c \ln x + b$

Here c and b are constants and 'ln' is the natural logarithm function.

Excel automatically calculates the logarithmic trend line for you once you applied it to your chart.

In the chart above the equation used to display the logarithmic trend line is:

$y = 22724\ln(x) + 39839$

Also note the R2 value of 0.9296 which is close to 1. This means that this trend line is very reliable.

Polynomial trend line

Use this trend line if there is fluctuation in your data.

The order of the polynomial is the number of fluctuations in the data or the number of bands (peak and valleys) appearing in a curve.

For example, use an order 2 polynomial trend line if there is only one hill or valley. Similarly use an order 3 polynomial trend line if there is one or two hills or valleys.

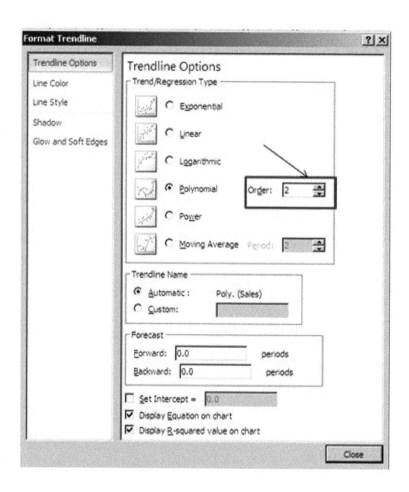

The following chart contains a polynomial trend line:

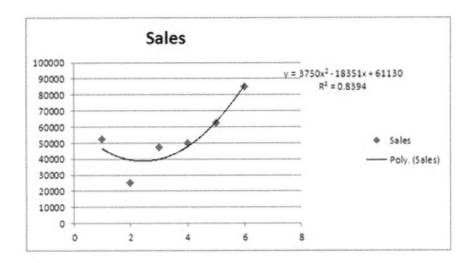

The equation used to calculate the polynomial trend line is:

$$y = b + c_1x + c_2x^2 + c_3x^3 + \ldots + c_6x^6$$

Here b and c1, c2, c6 are constants

Excel automatically calculates the polynomial trend line for you once you have applied it to your chart.

In the chart above the equation used to display the polynomial trend line is:

y = 3750 × 2 − 18351x + 61130

Also note the R2 value of 0.8394 which is close to 1. This means that this trend line is quite reliable.

Moving average trend line

Use this trend line if there is lot of fluctuation in your data.

Select the number of data points you want the trend line to average (by using the period option in Excel) and use as a point in the line.

For example, if you set the period to 2, then the average of the first two data points is used as the first point in the moving average trend line.

The average of the 2nd and 3rd data points is used as the second point in the trend line and so on.

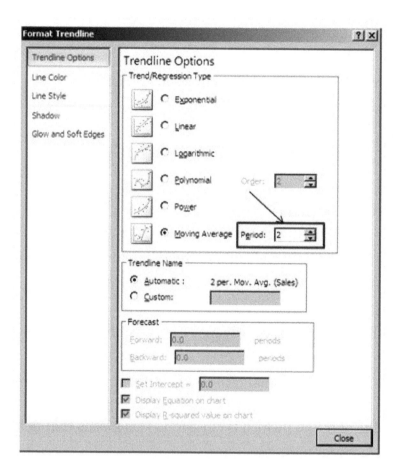

Moving average trend lines are generally used in stock analysis.

Generally low period values are used to show more immediate trends and high period values are used to show long term trends.

The following chart contains a moving average trend line:

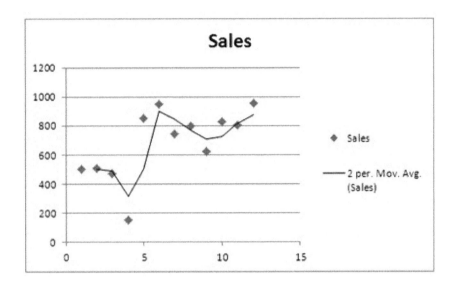

Note: The R2 value is not available with a moving average trend line.

Power trend line

Use this trend line if the data values increase at a specific rate. The following chart contains a power trend line:

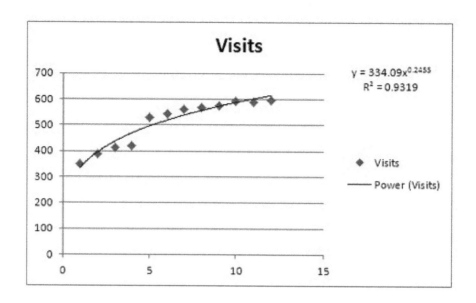

The equation used to calculate the power trend line is:

$$y = cx^b$$

Here c and b are constants.

Excel automatically calculates the power trend line for you once you have applied it to your chart.

In the chart above the equation used to display the power trend line is:

$y = 334.09 \times 0.2455$

Also note the R2 value of 0.9319 which is close to 1. This means that this trend line is very reliable.

Note: You cannot create a power trend line if your data contains zero or negative values.

Exponential trend line

Use this trend line if data values increase or decrease at increasingly higher rates. The following chart contains an exponential trend line:

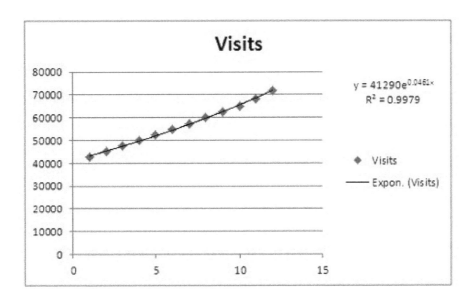

The equation used to calculate the exponential trend line is:

$$y = ce^{bx}$$

Here c and b are constants. e is the base of the natural logarithm.

Excel automatically calculates the exponential trend line for you once you have applied it to your chart.

In the chart above the equation used to display the exponential trend line is:

y = 41290e0.0461x

Also note the R2 value of 0.9979 which is very close to 1. This means that this trend line is very reliable.

Note: You cannot create an exponential trend line if your data contains zero or negative values.

Least square line

The trend line is also known as the least square line (or best fitting line) because Excel uses the method of least square to choose a trend line.

According to this method, Excel chooses that line as a trend line which minimizes the sum of squared vertical distances from each point to the line.

The vertical distance from each point to the line is called residual (or error).

As discussed earlier, each data point has one residual:

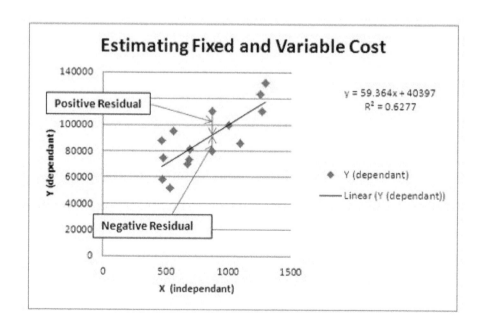

A positive error means a data point is above the least square line and a negative error means a data point is below the least square line.

Another definition of residual:

A residual (denoted by e) is the difference between the observed value and the predicted value of a dependant variable in regression analysis.

> *Residual (e)*
> *= observed value – predicted value*

Forecasting with trend lines

Forecasting with trend lines is one of the easiest ways of running regression analysis in Excel.

All you have to do is select the best trend line for your data and then enter the number of periods for which you want to forecast the data in the 'forecast forward' text box of the 'format trend line' dialog box:

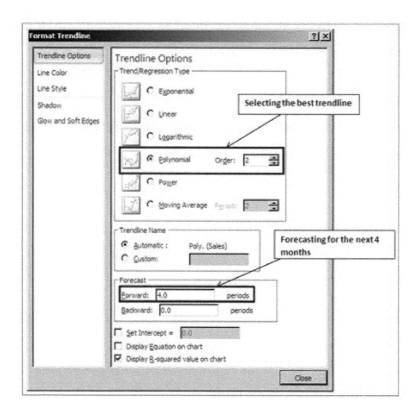

The chart below uses a trend line that is forecasting four months ahead and is clearly showing a trend towards an increase in sales:

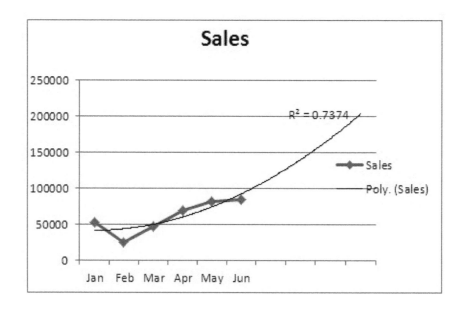

By using regression analysis, we have extended the trend line in the chart beyond the actual data to predict future values of the dependant variable (sales).

Note: You can also do **backward forecasting** by entering the number of periods for which you want to forecast the data in the 'forecast backward' text box of the 'format trend line' dialog box.

Running linear regression

In the case of linear regression we use only one independent variable (x) to predict the value of a dependent variable (y).

Let us suppose we want to predict sales from AOV (average order value). Therefore sales becomes the dependent variable and AOV becomes the independent variable. Now follow the steps below:

Step 1: Collect the data for both sales and AOV over a period of three or more months and then put the data in a table in Excel:

	f_x	=CORREL(C3:C18,D3:D18)
	C	D
	AOV	Sales
	1260	123118
	1007	99601
	1296	132000
	873	80000
	532	52000
	476	58625
	482	74624
	1273	110000
	692	81000
	690	73507
	564	95024
	470	88004
	675	70000
	870	110253
	1100	86000
Correlation Coefficient		0.792282266

Step 2: Determine the nature of the relationship (linear or nonlinear) between AOV and sales by graphing the data points using an Excel scatter chart so that the independent variable (AOV) is on the x axis and the dependent variable (sales) is on the y-axis:

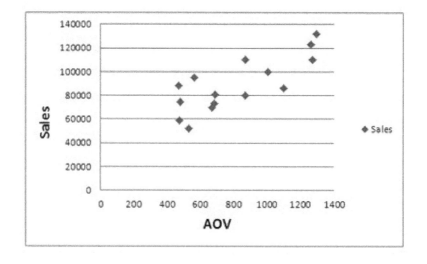

Step 3: Determine the correlation between AOV and sales.

If there is no or weak linear relationship between two variables or in other words the correlation between the two variables is zero or weak then this relationship is not good enough to predict anything. Therefore there is no point in running a regression analysis.

The correlation coefficient between AOV and sales according to the CORREL function turned out to be 0.79 which is a strong positive correlation. Hence we are in a position to predict the value of sales from AOV. In other words we can run regression analysis.

Step 4: Add the best trend line to your chart. From the chart above we can see that the relationship between AOV and sales forms a straight line.

In other words the relationship is linear. So the trend line that will best fit the data is linear trend line:

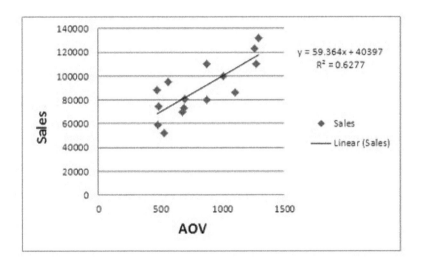

The formula used to calculate the linear trend line is:

$y = 59.364x + 40397$

Here y is the dependant variable (sales) and x is the independent variable (AOV).

The slope of the trend line is 59.36 which indicates that as AOV increases by $1 the sales increases by $59.36.

The number '40397' is the y-intercept which can be interpreted as monthly fixed sales. So even if AOV during a month is zero, this graph estimates that the business will still generate a sales of $40,397 a month.

The R2 value is 0.63 which indicates that 63% of the variation in monthly sales can be predicted from the variation in AOV.

This implies that the remaining 37% (100-63) variation in monthly sales can be predicted by other factors. We need to run multiple regression to determine other factors which influence the sale.

We can now calculate the predicted sales for each AOV by using the formula y = 59.364x + 40397 in our spreadsheet like this:

	D4	▾	f_x = (59.364*B4 +40397)	
	A	B	C	D
1				
2				
3		AOV	Sales	Predicted Sales
4		1260	123118	115195.64
5		1007	99601	100176.548
6		1296	132000	117332.744
7		873	80000	92221.772
8		532	52000	71978.648
9		476	58625	68654.264
10		482	74624	69010.448
11		1273	110000	115967.372
12		692	81000	81476.888
13		690	73507	81358.16
14		564	95024	73878.296
15		470	88004	68298.08
16		675	70000	80467.7
17		870	110253	92043.68
18		1100	86000	105697.4

Step 5: Calculate residuals for each data point. As stated earlier, a residual (denoted by e) is the difference between the observed value and predicted value of a dependant variable in regression analysis. Each data point has one residual:

E4		fx	=C4-D4	
	A	B	C	D	E
---	---	---	---	---	---
1					
2					
3		AOV	Sales	Predicted Sales	Residuals
4		1260	123118	115195.64	7922.36
5		1007	99601	100176.548	-575.548
6		1296	132000	117332.744	14667.256
7		873	80000	92221.772	-12221.772
8		532	52000	71978.648	-19978.648
9		476	58625	68654.264	-10029.264
10		482	74624	69010.448	5613.552
11		1273	110000	115967.372	-5967.372
12		692	81000	81476.888	-476.888
13		690	73507	81358.16	-7851.16
14		564	95024	73878.296	21145.704
15		470	88004	68298.08	19705.92
16		675	70000	80467.7	-10467.7
17		870	110253	92043.68	18209.32
18		1100	86000	105697.4	-19697.4

Step 6: Calculate the standard error of regression (SER).

SER is a measure of the accuracy of your predictions. It measures the spread of the data points around the least square line.

The function that is used to calculate the standard error of regression in Excel is STEYX:

STEYX (yrange, xrange)

Here yrange contains the values of the dependent variable, and xrange contains the values of the independent variable:

	F4			f_x	=STEYX(C4:C18,B4:B18)	

	A	B	C	D	E	F
1						
2						
3		AOV	Sales	Predicted Sales	Residuals	Standard Error of Regression
4		1260	123118	115195.64	7922.36	14467.26018
5		1007	99601	100176.548	-575.548	
6		1296	132000	117332.744	14667.256	
7		873	80000	92221.772	-12221.772	
8		532	52000	71978.648	-19978.648	
9		476	58625	68654.264	-10029.264	
10		482	74624	69010.448	5613.552	
11		1273	110000	115967.372	-5967.372	
12		692	81000	81476.888	-476.888	
13		690	73507	81358.16	-7851.16	
14		564	95024	73878.296	21145.704	
15		470	88004	68298.08	19705.92	
16		675	70000	80467.7	-10467.7	
17		870	110253	92043.68	18209.32	
18		1100	86000	105697.4	-19697.4	

According to descriptive statistics rule of thumb: you would expect about 68% of your predictions to be accurate within one standard error of regression (SER) and about 95% of your predictions to be accurate within two standard errors.

Any prediction/forecast that differs from the actual value by more than two standard errors is considered as an outlier (extreme value).

In our case, one standard error of regression is 14467.26. Therefore the two standard error of regression will be 14467.26 * 2 = 28934.52.

So according to descriptive statistics rule of thumb, 68% of the residuals (or errors) should be 14467.26 or smaller and 95% of the residuals (or errors) should be 28934.52 or smaller.

If you look at the residuals in column E, you can see that 12 residuals out of 15 or 80% of the residuals are equal or smaller than 14467.26 (i.e. within one standard error of regression).

Similarly 15 residuals out of 15 or 100% of the residuals are equal or smaller than 28934.52 (i.e. within two standard error of regression).

This means we could expect 80% of our predictions to be accurate within one standard error of regression (SER) and about 100% of our predictions to be accurate within two standard errors.

If we look at the first observation, the residual of $7,922.36 indicates that the predicted sales of $115,195.64 is too low by $7,922.36.

Running multiple regression

When we use two or more independent variables to predict the value of a dependent variable this type of regression is known as multiple regression.

Let us suppose we want to predict sales from AOV (average order value) and the number of ecommerce transactions. So sales becomes the dependent variable and AOV and the number of ecommerce transactions become independent variables.

Follow the steps below:

Step 1: Collect the data for both sales and AOV over a period of three or more months and then put the data in a table in Excel like the one below:

AOV	Transactions	Sales
1260	98	123118
1007	99	99601
1296	102	132000
873	92	80000
532	98	52000
476	123	58625
482	155	74624
1273	86	110000
692	117	81000
690	107	73507
564	168	95024
470	187	88004
675	104	70000
870	127	110253
1100	78	86000

Step 2: Click on the 'data' tab, then 'data analysis' to open the 'data analysis tool'. In the data analysis dialog box, select 'regression' from the list and click on the 'ok' button:

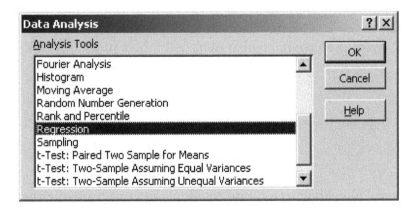

Note: You will need to install the Analysis ToolPak (an Excel add-in) in order to run multiple regression analysis in Excel. This tool pack is available in Excel 2007 and above versions.

Step 3: Enter the 'input Y range' and 'input X range'.

The input Y range contains all the values of a dependant variable (in this case sales).

The input X range contains all the values of independent variables (in this case AOV and transactions).

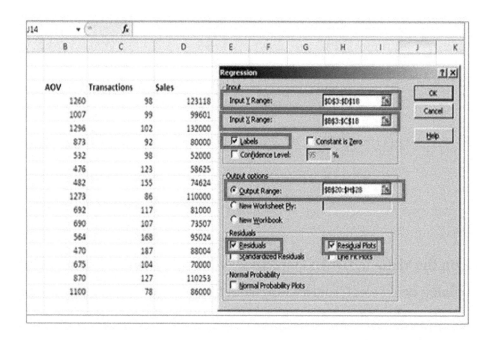

Select the 'labels' checkbox as we have also included labels in the input Y range and input X ranges.

Select the output range i.e. the cells where you want to display the results of multiple regression analysis.

Click on the 'residuals' checkbox to include residuals in your multiple regression analysis report.

Click on the 'residual plots' checkbox to include residual plots in your multiple regression analysis report.

Then click on the 'ok' button.

You will now see the output of your multiple regression analysis. It will look something like this:

SUMMARY OUTPUT

Regression Statistics	
Multiple R	0.976037919
R Square	0.95265002
Adjusted R Square	0.944758357
Standard Error	5370.16033
Observations	15

ANOVA

	df	SS	MS	F	Significance F
Regression	2	6962566143	3.48E+09	120.716	1.12699E-08
Residual	12	346063463.7	28838622		
Total	14	7308629607			

	Coefficients	Standard Error	t Stat	P-value	Lower 95%	Upper 95%	Lower 95.0%	Upper 95.0%
Intercept	-54398.47557	11217.98917	-4.84922	0.000399	-78840.3743	-29956.57683	-78840.3743	-29956.57683
AOV	96.93621799	6.268573272	15.46384	2.74E-09	83.27817012	110.5942659	83.27817012	110.5942659
Transactions	552.4142186	60.8742071	9.074684	1.01E-06	419.7807152	685.047722	419.7807152	685.047722

RESIDUAL OUTPUT

Observation	Predicted Sales	Residuals
1	121719.043	1398.956959
2	97854.83476	1746.165236
3	127495.2741	4504.725899
4	80848.99335	-848.9933547
5	51166.96716	833.032845
6	59779.47421	-1154.474209
7	77850.42186	-3226.421856
8	116735.4729	-6735.472939
9	77342.58917	3657.410829
10	71337.24233	2169.757665
11	93345.55264	1678.447364
12	94596.9956	-6592.9956
13	68320.87202	1679.127976
14	99942.15459	10310.84541
15	95420.11222	-9420.112221

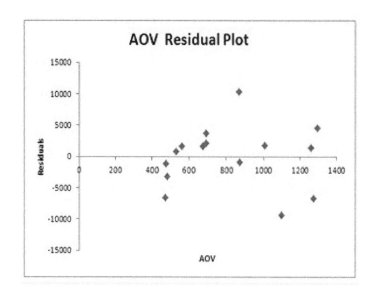

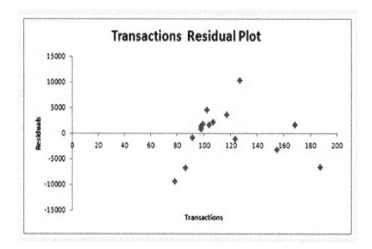

One of the most important output of a multiple regression analysis is the R2 value.

If you look at the R2 (or R square) value, it is 0.95 which is pretty close to 1.

The Adjusted R2 value is 0.94 which is a more reliable statistics as it takes into account your sample size (i.e. number of observations).

The adjusted R2 value of 0.94 indicates that 94% of the variation in monthly sales can be predicted from the variation in AOV and number of transactions.

This implies that the remaining 6% (100-94) variation in monthly sales can be predicted by other factors.

If you remember, when we ran linear regression our R2 value was 0.63. Which means that we were able to explain only 63% of the variation in monthly sales. With the R2 value of 0.94 we now can explain up to 94% variation in monthly sales. This is the advantage of running multiple regression.

 In the real world a single independent variable is rarely responsible for causing all of the variation in a dependant variable. Therefore most of the time you will find yourself running multiple regression.

> *The formula used by Excel to calculate the multiple regression is*
> $Y = a + b_1X_1 + b_2X_2$

Here y is the dependant variable (in this case sales).

X1 and X2 are the values of the independent variable (in this case AOV and number of transactions).

a is the y-intercept.

b1 is the slope of AOV and b2 is the slope of transactions.

You can see the values of a, b1 and b2 in the table below which shows the first output of multiple regression analysis:

	Coefficients	Standard Error	t Stat	P-value
Intercept	-54398.47557	11217.98917	-4.84922	0.000399
AOV	96.93621799	6.268573272	15.46384	2.74E-09
Transactions	552.4142186	60.8742071	9.074684	1.01E-06

So here the y-intercept is -54398.47, 'b1' is 96.94 and 'b2' is 552.41.

So the equation of multiple regression (or the **best prediction equation**) is:

$$y = -54398.47 + 96.94X1 + 552.41X2$$

By using this formula Excel calculated the predicted sales for each observation as shown above under the 'predicted sales' column. You can also see the residuals for each observation/data point.

The standard error of regression (SER) which measures the accuracy of our predictions is 5370.16 (see the first output of multiple regression analysis i.e. summary output).

Now according to descriptive statistics rule of thumb you would expect about **68%** of your predictions to be accurate within one standard error of regression and about **95%** of your predictions to be accurate within two standard errors.

Any prediction/forecast that differs from the actual value by more than two standard errors is considered as an outlier (extreme value)

In our case, one standard error of regression is 5370.16. Therefore the two standard error of regression will be 5370.16 * 2 = 10740.32.

So according to descriptive statistics rule of thumb, 68% of the residuals (or errors) should be 5370.16 or smaller and 95% of the residuals (or errors) should be 10740.32 or smaller.

So if you look at the residuals column in the second output of multiple regression (i.e. residual output), you can see that 14 residuals out of 15 or 93% of the residuals are equal or smaller than 5370.16 (i.e. within one standard error of regression).

Similarly 15 residuals out of 15 or 100% of the residuals are equal or smaller than 10740.32 (i.e. within two standard error of regression).

That means we could expect 93% of our predictions to be accurate within one standard error of regression (SER) and about 100% of our predictions to be accurate within two standard errors.

The last two outputs of multiple regressions (AOV residual plot and transactions residual plot) are residual plots which were explained earlier.

The p-value

When you run regression analysis, each independent variable has a p-value between 0 and 1.

> *The p-value is the probability that the results occurred randomly.*

If the p-value of an independent variable is less than or equal to 0.05 then it is considered to be useful for predicting the dependent variable.

Thus, the smaller the p-value, the higher the predictive power of the independent variable.

	Coefficients	Standard Error	t Stat	P-value
Intercept	-54398.47557	11217.98917	-4.84922	0.000399
AOV	96.93621799	6.268573272	15.46384	2.74E-09
Transactions	552.4142186	60.8742071	9.074684	1.01E-06

In the table above, you can see that the p-values of the independent variables 'AOV' and 'transactions' are very small: 2.742E-09 and 1.0E-06.

Since these p-values are less than 0.05 they are considered to be very useful for predicting the value of dependant variable (in this case 'sales').

Note: You can also use the Excel LINEST function to run multiple regression in Excel.

Predictive analytics process

That was a lot of statistics, wasn't it? Finally, we are in a position where we can carry out predictive analytics techniques.

I use the following process to do predictive analytics:

Step 1: Collect data and extract information from it - All modern day web analytics tools are able to collect data (i.e. visits, pageviews etc.) and extract considerable amount of information from it (i.e. goal conversion rate, visitor behaviour etc.).

You need to collect at least three months of performance data before you start trend analysis. Always strive to collect accurate data. If your data is not accurate than predictions will not be accurate either.

Step 2: Identify trends to analyse - Review your KPIs, especially the ones which drive revenue and cost, in order to determine the performance data you want to analyse and compare. For example, when reviewing the sales performance of your company you would analyse KPIs like conversions volume, conversion rate and average order value.

Step 3: Choose threshold - Define the level at which a variation is worth investigating. For example, a 30% increase or decrease in sales over a period of time should be worth investigating. Use historical data to choose threshold.

Step 5: Chart the data and add the best trend line to the chart.

Step 6: Analyse and interpret the data and spot patterns.

Step 7: Conduct cause analysis – Investigate why the variation occurred so that you can use this information to discount certain peaks or valleys in your data trends.

Step 8: Conduct regression analysis.

Lesson 18: Correlation and causation

Correlation is a statistical measurement of relationship between two variables.

Let us suppose that A and B are two variables. If, as A goes up, B goes up then A and B are positively correlated.

However, if as A goes up, B goes down then A and B are negatively correlated.

Causation is the theory that something happened as a result.

For example, a fall in temperature increased the sales of hot drinks.

The most important correlations that I have found so far are:

1. Negative correlation between conversion rate and average order value.

2. Negative correlation between conversion rate and transactions.

3. Positive correlation between conversion rate and acquisition cost.

These three correlations have completely changed the way I think about conversion optimization for good.

The whole conversion optimization process is based on correlation analysis.

367

Correlation based observations help you in coming up with a hypothesis. This is the hypothesis without which you cannot conduct any statistical tests and thus improve conversions.

As you learned earlier, correlation is also widely used in predictive analytics and predictive marketing. Before you can predict the value of a dependant variable from an independent variable, you first need to prove that the correlation between two variables is not weak or zero. Otherwise such a relationship is not good to predict anything.

Correlation does not imply causation

Correlation means there is a mere presence of a relationship between two variables/events. It does not imply that one causes the other.

For example, we cannot automatically assume that an increase in social media shares has resulted in an improvement in search engine rankings.

Before we can prove there is a correlation between social media shares and rankings, we first need to prove that a linear relationship exist between social shares and rankings i.e. any increase or decrease in the value of social shares causes a corresponding increase or decrease in search engine ranking.

Without first proving a linear relationship, you could end up forming and testing the wrong hypothesis.

Once you have proved the correlation between social shares and rankings you then determine the correlation coefficient to measure the strength and direct of this linear relationship.

If the linear relationship is strong then you go ahead and conduct regression analysis to predict the value of one variable from another.

Needless to say, correlation and regression are two strong pillars of conversion optimization and are very important for you as a digital marketer.

Lesson 19: Analysing data trends

Analysing data trends is an age old powerful tactic which is used to measure the performance of marketing campaigns over time and to predict future outcomes.

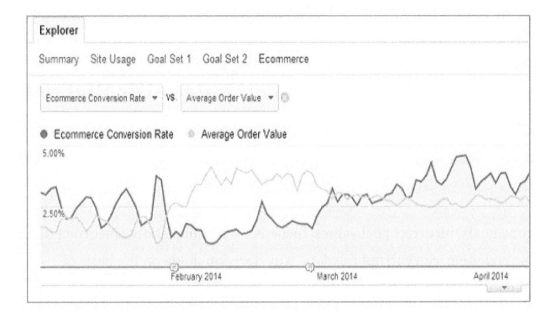

We complete trend analysis in order to answer questions like:

1. What are my top selling products?

2. What are my top converting keywords?

3. Which keywords should I bid on?

4. Where should I invest my money and resources to get the highest possible ROI?

5. Which is the most effective marketing channel in terms of goal conversions and revenue?

In trend analysis we spot a pattern(s), interpret it and then make predictions on the basis of historical data.

How you analyse and interpret the 'data trends' plays a very important role in optimizing your marketing campaigns and making predictions about future outcomes.

Just one wrong interpretation and you can end up losing hundreds of thousands of pounds (depending upon the size of your business).

Following are the key rules for analysing 'data trends' to get the highest possible ROI from your marketing campaigns:

Rule 1: Always question how the data is collected

Before you analyse and interpret any data, always make sure that the data has been collected as accurately as possible especially for the time period you have chosen to analyse.

Often wrong goals, incorrect goal values, incorrect ROI calculations, incorrect deployment of tracking codes etc. can corrupt the data. Any decision made on the basis of corrupted data could prove fatal for your marketing efforts and business.

*If you are not really sure how the data has been collected or if you cannot purge it then avoid taking **major** business decisions on the basis of such data.*

Collect fresh data and then wait for at least three months before you start analysing data trends.

Rule 2: Understand that historical data is dated

The insight that you get from analysing historical data is often out of date and it does not always match with the present marketing conditions.

> *The older the data, the more unreliable it becomes.*

This is because we live and operate in a constant change of marketing conditions, trends, buying behaviour, pricing, competition and multi-channel funnels.

So comparing one year's web analytics data to the last years could be like comparing apples to oranges because so much would have changed during that time from website size, traffic, products, competitors and target market.

So the rule of thumb is, **do not over rely on historical data** especially when it is more than one year old.

Rule 3: Select the right time period to analyse your data trends

Get a deeper understanding of your business and its cycle of ups and downs. Understand your businesses 'sales cycle'.

> *Your business, just like any other business, tends to have natural ups and downs over the course of a year. These ups and downs are called **seasonality**.*

We can never really understand this seasonality if we do not compare last year's data with the present year's data.

This is one of the few situations where sales data that is more than one year old becomes important. You need to use this understanding of seasonality to select the right time period.

As a rule of thumb:

"One week does not make a data trend.

One month does not make a data trend.

Even two months does not make a data trend.

Three or more months makes a data trend."

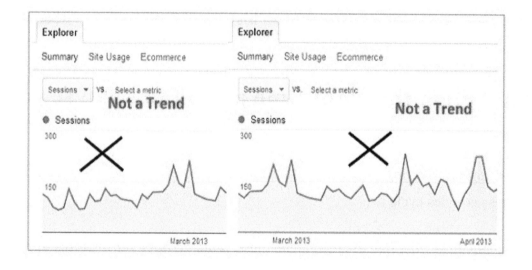

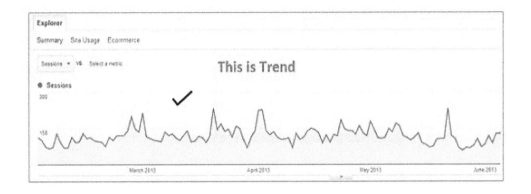

Rule 4: Add comparisons to your data trends

Comparison adds 'context' to data and makes it more meaningful.

You get a better understanding of a marketing campaign when you compare its performance with the past performance using two different date ranges.

Only through comparison can you find out whether you are making progress or regress over time.

For example look at the following one week traffic report:

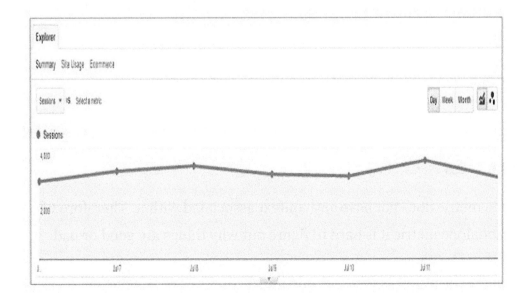

What insight do you get from this report?

Can you determine whether the traffic has increased or decreased in comparison to last week? No, you cannot.

For that you need to compare this data with last week data:

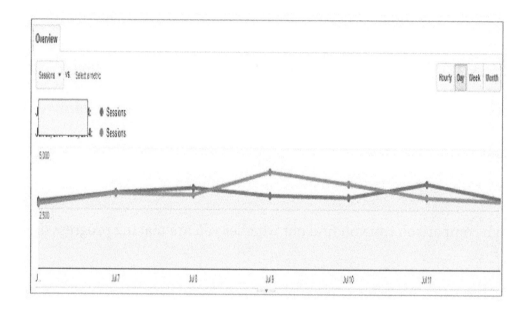

Now after looking at the report above, we can conclude that traffic has dropped a bit in comparison to last week.

You cannot get such types of insight without data comparison.

Rule 5: Never report a standalone metric in your data trends

A standalone metric does not have any context associated with it. Therefore when you report a standalone metric it is hard to figure out why things are good or bad.

For example, in the report below, the only metric that we see is 'revenue':

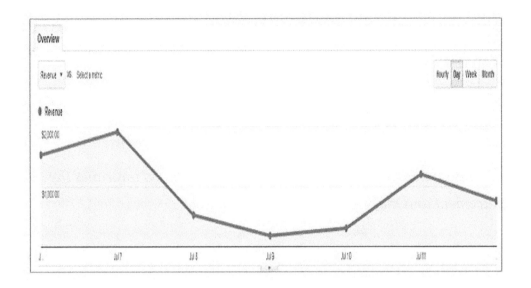

So we have no idea why the revenue declined so drastically in the middle of the week. We therefore need to add at least one more metric, in order to add context to our data trends:

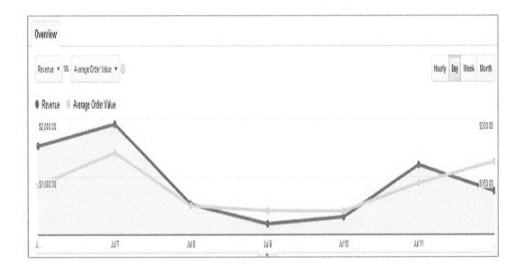

Now, from the report above, we can conclude that one of the reasons for the drastic drop in revenue was the drastic drop in average order value.

You will not get this level of insight if you report, only a single metric in your data trend.

Rule 6: Segment your data before you analyse/report data trends

Ask any analyst worth his salt which is the most important task in web analytics and he will tell you straightaway, that it is **data segmentation**.

> *Segmentation not only adds context to the data but also improves the measurement and make the data more actionable.*

For example, in the report below, we have no idea why the overall website traffic went down:

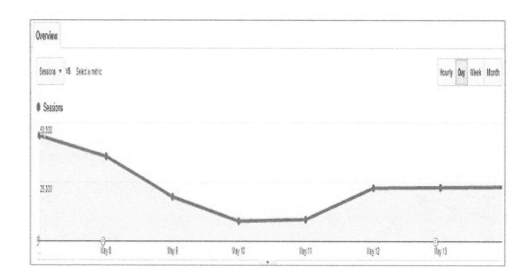

You need to segment this data trend in order to get a better insight:

378

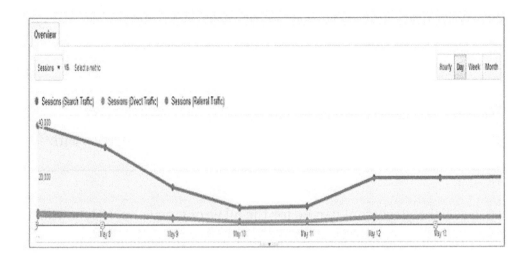

After segmenting the data trend, we can conclude that the decline in search traffic is the main reason for the decline in overall website traffic.

By segmenting this data trend further, we can figure out the role of organic search and paid search in the decline of the overall search traffic.

The more you can segment the data, the better the actions you can take.

Rule 7: Report something which impacts the business bottom-line

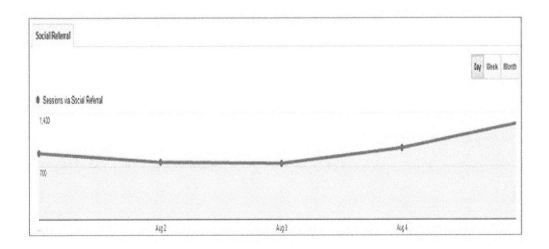

Does it really matter that 'sessions with social referrals' are going up?

Similarly, does it really matter that Facebook likes are increasing over time or Twitter followers are increasing?

The answer is 'no'. It does not really matter, unless you tie these metrics with **conversions.**

This is because social engagement can be for the all wrong reasons. Maybe you are engaging with random people who are not really your target audience. Maybe you are engaging with your competitors.

If this is not the case then your conversions must increase along with 'sessions with social referrals' over time and you must be able to prove it.

If you do not tie your metrics with conversions/transactions then you will not be able to report something that impacts the business bottom-line which can convince your client/boss to invest more money in your campaigns.

Rule 8: Spell out the insight

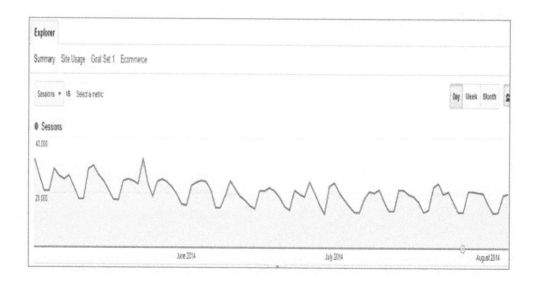

What can someone really understand through this data trend?

For an average person, the lines are going up and down. So what? Unless you are creating reports for yourself, you need to add context to it.

You can add context through:

    1. Comparison.

    2. The use of two or more metrics.

    3. Data segmentation.

You can also add context through the use of annotations, graphical elements (like arrows) and, above all, through written commentary.

By commentary I mean what **story** the data trend is really telling you.

Write at least four or five lines which describe what is going on, **in plain English**. Show how the trend is impacting the business bottom-line in **monetary terms.**

You need to explain the reason for big spikes and deep troughs in your data trends when you present it to the senior management/client.

Rule 9: Use sparklines

Region	Quarter 1	Quarter 2	Quarter 3	Quarter 4	Sales
North	£3,245	£3,567	£3,976	£4,021	£14,809
South	£2,120	£1,980	£1,743	£2,100	£7,943
East	£4,213	£4,589	£3,978	£3,500	£16,280
West	£2,130	£1,934	£1,543	£1,200	£6,807

A sparkline is a feature added in Microsoft Excel 2010 and beyond. It is a tiny chart embedded in a cell.

> *Through sparklines you can easily spot patterns in the data presented in a tabular format.*

You can enter text in a cell and at the same time use a sparkline as its background. Any change in data of a cell immediately changes its sparkline. So a sparkline is another way of adding context to the data.

Rule 10: Do not jump to conclusions

While doing trend analysis, it is very important to keep in mind that the data you are looking at is dated.

We live in a constant change of marketing conditions, trends, buying behavior, pricing, competition and multi-channel funnels.

> *History does not repeat itself in online marketing.*

It is highly unlikely that you can replicate your success rate by carrying out the exact same tasks you executed six months ago with a particular campaign.

A major Google update or the arrival of a new and powerful competitor can easily screw the predictions you have made about your outcomes (on the basis of trend analysis).

So you need to keep several factors in mind while drawing conclusions from data trends and not just the metrics you are analysing in your trends.

Rule 11: Understand the manipulation of the y-axis and data points

This is a pretty common data visualization trick I often see in action.

Check out this chart which measures Facebook fan growth of a website:

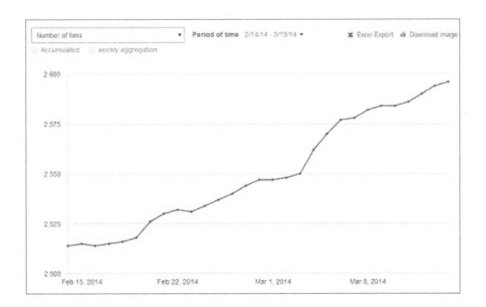

One look at this chart and it looks like Facebook fan growth has skyrocketed in the last one month. But if you look closely, you can see that the y-axis does not start at zero, it starts at 2500.

Actually in the last one month, the Facebook fan base increased from 2514 to 2596. That is a 3.26% increase in fan base. But by truncating the y-axis and starting it from 2500, it looks the fan base has increased by several thousand percent.

Now if I draw the same chart with y-axis starting at 0, then you will see a completely different picture:

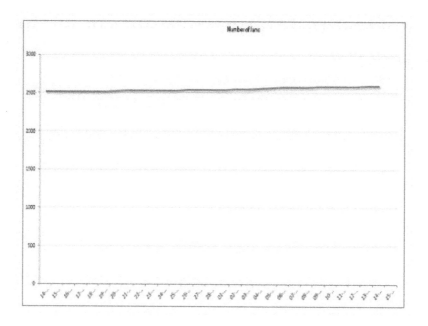

That does not as good. Does it?

Let me amplify this change by starting the y-axis at 2514 and ending it at 2596 and at same time plotting just two data points (the very first 2514 and the very last 2596):

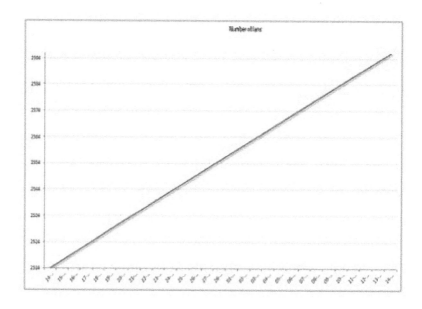

Now it looks like a truly phenomenal growth chart. Doesn't it?

Note how by plotting just two data points I have managed to remove any fluctuation (peak, valley) in the data trend. Now from the chart it looks like there has been a steady sharp growth in Facebook fan base.

The same data visualization trick can be applied to column charts as well to amplify changes:

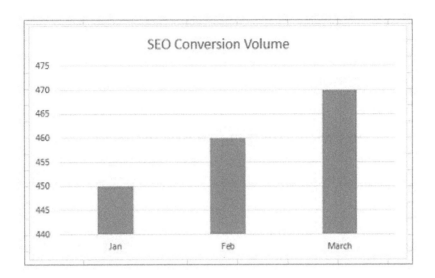

Here the conversion volume through an SEO campaign has increased by only 4% in the last three months. But when you look at the chart, the change in conversion volume looks much bigger.

Here is how this change actually looks:

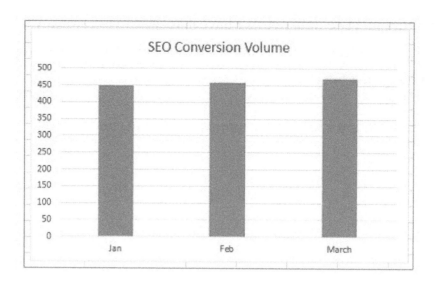

Another data visualization trick is to hide the scale on the y-axis:

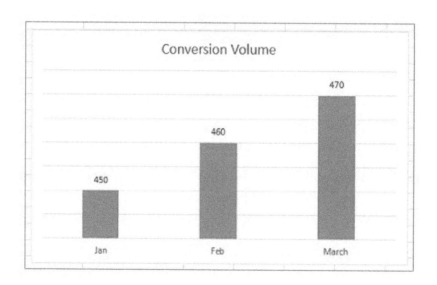

Without any scale on the y-axis, there is no way of knowing where the y-axis starts from.

Takeaways

1. Always check your chart for a truncated y-axis.
2. Always check your chart for hidden scales.
3. Do not trust charts that contain just a few data points.
4. Statistics can be misleading depending on how they are presented.

Lesson 20: 80/20 rule

According to the **Pareto Principal** (also known as the 80–20 rule), 80% of the effect come from 20% of the cause which means:

1. 80% of your sales comes from 20% of your websites visitors.
2. 80% of your output comes from 20% of your input.
3. 80% of your sales comes from 20% of your products.
4. 80% of your profit comes from 20% of your products.

So what you need to do is determine those '20% of everything' and work relentlessly on them.

You cannot sell each and every one of your client's products in each and every location of your country. Do not spread your marketing efforts and resources too thin by trying to be visible everywhere for every single product you sell.

Let us imagine that your target market is the United States. Your average customer can be anywhere from the US. Let us also suppose that after analysing one years' worth of data, you found out that people from New York City buy two times more than an average visitor to your website. Imagine they tend to spend 30% more than the average per order.

Now you know where your best customers live:

	New York City Clients (Best Clients)	Average Clients (can be anywhere from US)
No. of transactions/year	4000	2000
Average order value	$70	$40
Total Revenue	$280000	$80000
Total Spend	$36000	$50000
Gross Profit	$244000	$30000

That is why the best customers generate more profit than average or low value customers.

Your cost per acquisition will be high if you target the whole of the US through search marketing or any other ad campaigns. It is pretty obvious that your total spend is going to be higher for acquiring average clients.

By directing your marketing efforts in acquiring more profitable clients, you can increase your revenue and profit without increasing traffic or spending more on content creation and marketing.

Now the big questions that comes up are: Why are people from New York City our best clients? What are they purchasing? What can we do so that they buy more?

If you can get answers to these questions you can increase your sales within a few weeks without increasing website traffic or spending more on content marketing. This should be your aim as a marketer.

You need to learn to answer 'why?' if you wish you to remain in business for the foreseeable future. One of the most critical piece in today's web analytics is answering 'why?' Why do people do what they do on your website?

For example,

> *Why people buy products from your website?*
> *Why people do not buy products from your website?*
> *What should you do so that people buy products from your website?*

The answer is not 'increase the traffic'. The answer is 'ask your visitors' and 'know your target audience'. Spend lot of your time and resources in getting answers to these 'why?' questions.

The law of diminishing returns and your marketing budget

According to the law of diminishing returns:

> *If you keep adding more of one unit of production to a productive process while keeping all others units constant, you will at some point produce lower per unit returns.*

For example, if you keep pumping more money into a Facebook campaign without changing the present form of the campaign, at some point you will reach the point of diminishing returns and once you cross this point, your conversion rate will go down and cost per acquisition will go up.

So when you are thinking of increasing the budget of a campaign by a considerable amount, think of putting more ads and targeting more keywords.

This way you will change multiple units of production and can stay away from the point of diminishing returns.

How to determine the point of diminishing returns?

To determine the point of diminishing returns you need to gradually add more of one unit of production into the production process.

If you rapidly add units, you will never know when you crossed the point of diminishing returns and started losing money. So what that means is that you need to gradually increase your budget.

Understand that just doubling the budget of a high performing campaign may not result in a proportional increase in performance. You need to do a lot more than just increasing the budget.

Run more ads, target more keywords or new markets to stay away from the point of diminishing returns. So now you know that you cannot double your sales just by doubling your marketing budget.

The law of diminishing returns and multi-channel marketing

Understand that if you are doing multi-channel marketing no one campaign is solely responsible for conversions and sales.

Different marketing channels work together to create sales and conversions.

Some marketing channels help more in assisting conversions than completing conversions. We call these channels **assisting marketing channels**. Other marketing channels help more in completing conversions.

So if you over invest in a particular marketing channel while overlooking the role of assisting marketing channels, you will reach the point of diminishing returns faster than you think.

In that case you are adding more of one unit of production (here budget) to one marketing channels while keeping other units constants (i.e. not investing a proportional amount in assisting marketing channels).

The law of diminishing returns and last click keywords optimization

In the same way that we have assisting marketing channels, we have **assisting keywords** in the case of PPC campaigns.

These keywords help more in assisting conversions than completing conversions. Similarly we have **last click keywords**. These are the keywords people searched for just before completing a conversion and are attributed conversions in a last click conversion model.

The average PPC marketer spends his life optimizing for last click keywords, assuming that only these keywords make up the whole conversion funnel. He completely ignore the role played by assisting keywords.

In the case of PPC, if you keep optimizing for last click keywords while ignoring the first and middle clicks keywords (collectively known as assisting keywords) you will at some point produce lower per unit returns.

That means your cost per acquisition from PPC campaigns at some point will start rising and your profit on sales will start declining.

Then the only way to remain within your cost per acquisition (CPA) targets is by tweaking (add, pause, delete, change bids) last click keywords. But this is a sub optimal way of optimizing a PPC campaign as you are only optimizing a small part of the conversion process.

So in order to strengthen your PPC campaigns you also need to **bid on keywords that initiate or assist conversions.** In this way you can stay away from the point of diminishing returns and remain within your CPA targets much longer.

The law of diminishing returns and last click CPA optimization

The CPA (cost per acquisition) that you see in your Google AdWords report or Google Analytics report is not your actual cost per acquisition. Sorry to disappoint you but it is actually the **cost per last click conversion**.

So if you ignore first and middle click keywords and optimize PPC campaigns on the basis of cost per last click conversions than you will not get optimal results from your campaigns and sometimes even lose money.

This is because if a keyword is not completing a sale, it may be initiating a sale or assisting a sale. If you stop bidding on it because it's cost per last click conversion (the so called CPA reported by Google AdWords) is too high or it is not completing any conversion then you may lose money.

The law of diminishing returns and the conversion optimization process

*Conversion optimization is the process of optimizing the **online performance** of a business.*

Conversion optimization encompasses any online and offline footprints as long as they can be measured, classified or categorized and are used to optimize the **online performance** of a business. Here there is a strong emphasis on optimizing the online performance.

Data can also be used to optimize the offline performance of a business and to take a wide range of business decisions, from operational to strategic.

For that we use other business intelligence technologies such as supply-chain analytics, predictive analytics, data mining etc. all of which are not conversion optimization. Conversion optimization cannot optimize management effectiveness or fix operational and strategic inefficiencies or underlying issues with your business model or pricing.

In order for a business to truly grow you need to optimize every aspect of your conversion funnel from initial lead generation to post sales follow up.

A conversion optimizer is not a business analyst. The difference between a conversion optimizer/digital analyst and a business analyst is not clear for many people.

While it is true that both conversion optimizers and business analysts share some common analytics tricks, there are a large number of analytics disciplines which fall only in the domain of a business analyst.

For example, a business analyst knows about and deals with supply chain analytics, predictive analytics, data mining, business process modelling, stake holder management etc. He/she often works in-house, has more control over day to day business operations and marketing activities and deals directly with key stakeholders.

Unlike conversion optimizers, business analysts optimize the whole business process from operational to strategic. In many companies' conversion optimizers often work alongside business analysts and/or report to business analysts.

So it is important to understand what a conversion optimizer can do and what they cannot do for your business. Many folks do not understand this difference and expect a conversion optimizer to work in the capacity of a business analyst, and that too from a remote location, which is not really possible.

Business analysts have got an entirely different skillset to conversion optimizers and need to be hired and trained in-house.

So, in the grand scheme of things, the whole conversion optimization process is just one unit of production. If you keep adding more of one unit of production to a productive process while keeping all others units constant, you will at some point produce lower per unit returns.

What that means is; if all you are doing to improve your business bottom-line is relying solely on your service provider to optimize your website for conversions then according to the law of diminishing returns you will not get very far in your chosen business.

You need to do a lot more than just optimizing your website for conversion. You need to work on improving management effectiveness and fixing operational and strategic inefficiencies.

The law of diminishing returns and market budget allocation

A data driven marketer has to face a lot of questions and challenges while allocating marketing budgets. Some of the most common questions are:

1. Can I double my sales just by doubling my marketing budget?

2. Why do I see a decline in the conversion rate and an increase in cost per acquisition when I rapidly invest huge amount of money?

3. What will happen if I over invest in one marketing channel and side-line other marketing channels because their last click conversions are not good?

4. Why does the performance of a campaign sometimes deteriorate once I start pumping more money into it?

Let us imagine that, because it is performing so well, you increase the budget of a PPC campaign by 80% (all other things being constant) but instead of getting better results you start seeing a decline in the conversion rate and an increase in the cost per acquisition.

I have been in this situation myself several times. I saw a campaign performing very well, got excited and increased its budget by 80-100% the next month and then... BAM! The conversion rate went down and the cost per acquisition went up along with my panic and fear.

Recently one of my clients was similarly excited. He was amazed by the performance of his Facebook campaign over the last three months and asked me to double the ad spend.

Having been burned several times in the past by investing too much at once in the wrong way, I knew that this was not going to work. So I did what marketers usually do and convinced him that this was not a good idea and that we needed to **go slow**.

I want you to think and plan before increasing investment in any marketing channel just because **it is performing well**.

Although the high performance seems a justifiable reason to invest more, things are not that black and white in a multi-channel online environment and overlooking important factors can result in a massive loss in revenue especially if you are investing tens of thousands of dollars.

Before you invest more money in any marketing channel you need to look at the following two factors:

1. The law of diminishing returns.
2. The role of assisting marketing channels.

According to the law of diminishing returns, if you keep adding more of one unit of production to a productive process while keeping all others units constant, you will at some point produce lower per unit returns.

For example, if you keep pumping more money into an AdWords campaign without changing the present form of the campaign, at some point you will reach the point of diminishing returns and once you cross this point your conversion rate will go down and cost per acquisition will go up.

When you are thinking of increasing the budget of a PPC campaign by a considerable amount, think instead of putting more ads and targeting more keywords. In this way you will change multiple units of production and can stay away from the point of diminishing returns.

You also need to understand the role of assisting marketing channels.

Let's imagine that up until now you are investing in an AdWords campaign with the belief that it is generating a lot of revenue and has a high conversion rate. But before you over invest in AdWords, let us wait a minute and ask some questions:

Do you really think the AdWords campaign is generating all those revenues and conversions especially in this world of multi-channel marketing where every marketing channel assist in conversions in some way?

Are you completely sure there are no other marketing channels which are helping in driving the AdWords conversions?

You need to look at the role played by assisting marketing channels before you take big decisions and double/triple the budget of a very successful campaign in a hope to multiply its performance.

If you do not, you may reach the point of diminishing returns as you are adding more of one unit of production (in this case budget) to one marketing channel while keeping other units constants (i.e. not investing proportional amount in assisting marketing channels).

This theory holds true for any campaign/marketing channel and not just AdWords.

Takeaways

1. Understand that just doubling the budget of a high performing campaign may not result in a proportional increase in performance. You need to do a lot more than just increasing the budget. Consider running more ads, targeting more keywords or new markets to stay away from the point of diminishing returns.

2. Go slow with your investment in any marketing campaign/channel in its present form. If you rapidly invest huge amounts of money, you will never know when you crossed the point of diminishing returns and started losing money.

3. Understand that no one campaign is solely responsible for conversions and sales if you are doing multi-channel marketing.

4. Understand that over investing in any marketing channel while overlooking the role of assisting marketing channels may take you to the point of diminishing returns faster than you think.

Lesson 21: Making the switch from traffic to conversions

"For many of us, the number one way to increase sales and leads is to send more traffic to the website".

Here lies the problem. As you acquire more traffic through different marketing channels (organic, PPC, email, social media etc.) you need to spend more time and resources on content development and marketing.

Then at some point you realize that your company spends way too much on acquisitions (conversions).

By the way, have you ever calculated cost per acquisition for your organic search campaigns? If not, then you should.

We all know the conversion rate of our websites. But what do we do about it?

"Many of us tend to live in a world where the conversion rate is a universal constant and all we can do is increase the traffic".

More traffic means more sales. But it also means more ad spend.

Let us suppose you have got a new client. What can you do to increase the revenue of his website? You have got two options here:

1. Create more content, target new keywords and effectively use social media for links acquisition. Which we all do but most of the time we ignore CPA and lifetime value.

2. Focus more on finding out why people do not buy from your website and what you can do about it. **This is the recommended option.**

Conversion optimization is all about improving the sales and conversions of a website without increasing the ad spend and/or traffic. It is all about getting the most out of our existing traffic.

You can save a lot of time and money on content development, marketing and traffic acquisition by running conversion driven campaigns instead of traffic driven campaigns. All of this may sound obvious to me and you, but we still do not focus much on improving the conversion rate of a website or lifetime value of a visitor.

We tend to overlook the conversion optimization process and spend the majority of our time in acquiring more traffic through keyword research, content development and marketing.

The traffic driven approach is hurting your business

When you work with the mind-set of just increasing traffic to drive sales:

1. You are not always acquiring the best customers through your marketing campaigns.
2. You are most likely acquiring low value customers who buy once or twice maximum in their lifetime.
3. You are not spending enough on acquiring the most profitable customers and thus loosing big on revenue and net profit.

When you focus on improving the conversion rate of your website, you get the best customers because you are doing two things better:

1. Targeting the right people.

2. Ensuring that the right people buy.

"Traffic driven campaigns will sooner or later come back to haunt you"

Traffic acquisition is becoming more expensive and challenging with each passing month/year due to a rise in labour cost, advertising competition and market saturation. At some point your cost per acquisition may become so high that you will no longer be profitable and may go out of business.

On the other hand:

"Conversion driven campaigns reduce acquisition cost, increase customer lifetime value and increase website traffic."

Conversion driven campaigns will not only reduce your cost per acquisition over time, thus making you more and more profitable, but it will also increase customer lifetime value and increase your website traffic.

You may ask how a conversion driven campaign will increase website traffic. Well, your conversion rate is not going to increase on its own. It is going to increase only when you are providing something of value to your target audience and you are getting better and better in providing such value over time.

The more value you provide to your target audience, the more customers you will attract. More satisfied customers mean higher customer lifetime value, more word of mouth publicity, more recommendations, more social mentions and thus higher traffic volume.

Conversion driven campaigns are always profitable

"Conversion driven campaigns are always more profitable than traffic driven campaigns when it comes to increasing sales."

Let us suppose you own an ecommerce website which has got the following traffic statistics:

Average monthly visits = 10,000

Ecommerce Conversion Rate of the website = 0.25%

Average order value = £100

Now you want to increase your sales and you have got a monthly budget of £2,000.

You have got two options; you can either choose to spend this £2,000 on acquiring more traffic to increase sales or you can spend the same amount on conversion optimization to increase sales.

Option one: Increasing sales by acquiring more traffic

Let us suppose you choose to acquire more traffic with the aim to increase sales. After all, conventional wisdom dictates that more traffic equals more orders.

If you are spending £2,000 a month, then you would need at least £2,000 of additional sales in return just to break even (no profit, no loss)

Number of additional orders required for £2,000 sale

= Additional sales/average order value

= £2,000/100

= 20

So you would need 20 additional orders each month just to cover the cost of your marketing campaigns. Obviously you need much more than 20 orders in order to make profit.

In order to get a reasonable positive ROI of say 100% (meaning you spent x and earned 2x in revenue), you would need at least 40 additional orders each month from your marketing activities. Only then will you generate an ROI of 100% and additional sales of £4,000 (40 orders * £100 average order value) each month.

Additional traffic required to get 40 orders
= number of additional orders required to get 100% ROI / ecommerce conversion rate
= 40 / 0.25%
= 16,000 visits

So you need to increase your website traffic by **160%** ([26,000 – 10,000]/10,000 *100) to generate additional sales of £4,000 per month, provided the ecommerce conversion rate at least remains constant, if it does not decrease.

The 26,000 figure is derived by adding 10,000 of average monthly traffic and 16,000 of additional monthly traffic.

Average value of each additional visit to your website
= £4,000 / 16,000
= **£0.25**

We call this average value the **ecommerce per session value** which measures how valuable your website traffic is.

Now how long do you think it will take to increase the existing website traffic by 160%?

Let us suppose it takes six months (still a conservative figure).

So after six months you would have spent £12,000 (£2,000 * 6) in acquiring additional traffic to generate an additional £4,000 in monthly sales.

Option two: Increasing sales by improving conversion rate

Let us suppose you choose to increase only your conversion rate in order to increase sales and your monthly spend on conversion optimization is the same £2,000

Now in order to get a reasonably positive ROI of 100%, you need an additional 40 orders each month as calculated earlier.

Conversion rate required to get an additional 40 orders each month
= number of additional orders required/ present website traffic
= 40/10,000
= 0.40%

So if you increase your conversion rate from 0.25% to 0.40%, you will generate an additional 40 orders each month, provided your website traffic volume at least remains the same, if it does not increase.

Average value of each additional visit to your website
= £4,000 / 10,000
= **£0.40**

To summarise, in the case of the traffic driven campaign, the average value of each additional visit to your website is £0.25. In the case of the conversion driven campaign, the average value of each additional visit to your website is £0.40

So just by focusing on conversion optimization, you increased the ecommerce per session value by 60% ([0.4-0.25]/0.25 * 100])

When you focused on conversion optimization, your traffic became 60% more valuable for your business than when you focused only on traffic acquisition.

So how long do you think it will take to increase the ecommerce conversion rate to 0.40%?

Let us suppose it takes three months (a pretty realistic figure), after which you stopped the conversion optimization campaign.

So after six months you would have spent £6,000 (£2,000 * 3) to generate an additional £4,000 in monthly sales.

To summarise, in the case of the traffic driven campaign, you spent £12,000 in acquiring additional traffic in order to generate an additional £4,000 in monthly sales. In the case of the conversion driven campaign, you spent £6,000 in improving the conversion rate in order to generate an additional £4,000 in monthly sales.

So is the conversion driven campaign more profitable than the traffic driven campaign? **Absolutely.**

Now let us imagine that you did not stop your conversion optimization campaign and after six months your ecommerce conversion rate increased from 0.25% to 2% and your website traffic is still around 10,000 visits.

So with a 1.75 (2-0.25) percentage point increase in conversion rate and 10,000 traffic, you would be generating 175 (1.75% * 10,000) additional orders each month after six months.

If the average order value is still £100 (highly unlikely, as it should improve when you do conversion optimization), you would still be generating an additional sales of £17,500 (175 orders * £100 average order value) each month after six months.

So after six months you would have spent £12,000 (£2,000 * 6) to generate an additional £17,500 in monthly sales.

To summarise, in the case of a six month long traffic driven campaign, you spent £12,000 in acquiring additional traffic in order to generate an additional £4,000 in monthly sales.

In the case of a six month long conversion driven campaign, you spent £12,000 in improving conversion rate in order to generate an additional £17,500 in monthly sales.

So, is a conversion driven campaign more profitable than a traffic driven campaign? **Absolutely, I have proved this twice now.**

I have also proved to you that:

> *Conversion driven campaigns become progressively more profitable.*

The longer you run such campaigns, the more profitable you will become.

Conversion driven campaigns have a higher lifetime value than traffic driven campaigns

Even if you stop spending money on conversion optimization at some point, you will continue to get the benefit of an increase in ecommerce conversion rate for a very long time. This is not really the case with a traffic driven approach to increasing sales.

> *"Your traffic will always deteriorate much faster than your ecommerce conversion rate."*

If in doubt, switch off all of your paid marketing campaigns for the time being and you will get my point.

Other than that, the cost of acquiring new customers will always increase. As long as you stick to a traffic driven approach to increase sales, your cost per acquisition is only going to increase over time. It is not going to decrease.

At some point your cost per acquisition may become so high that advertising is no longer profitable for you.

> *"The lifetime value of a conversion driven approach to increasing sales and remaining profitable is much higher."*

Lesson 22: Making good marketing decisions

It took me a long time to understand that life does not need to be perfect before you can be happy. In the same way, you do not need perfect data before you can take perfect marketing decisions.

> *"If you seek perfection then the majority of the time you will find yourself unhappy because perfection happens only once in a while."*

Another downside of seeking perfection is **procrastination**.

If you spend the majority of your time trying to collect perfect data so that you can take that perfect business decision then there is a high probability that at the end of the day you will not take any decision/ action at all and taking timely decisions is so important in today's world of cut throat competition.

> *An imperfect decision is always better than no decision.*

Remember, no analytics tool is perfect. You cannot expect to get 100% accurate data from any analytics tool out there and Google Analytics is no exception. So avoid being obsessed with collecting the perfect data and be happy with good enough data.

Understand the business and get the 'context'

You should always start your analysis by assuming that you have no access to your client's GA account. Now how will you optimize the website for conversions?

Well, it is quite simple. Browse the client's website and ask tons of questions.

You do not really need GA or any other analytics tool to develop a great understanding of the client's business.

There is a common misconception that you can develop a great understanding of a business just by diving into the analytics reports. This is simply not true. GA reports are just huge collection of website usage data. They cannot spell out any insight on their own to you.

If you want to gain insight from the GA reports then you need to know the context beforehand. This is the context in which you will eventually collect, analyze and interpret the GA data or any data and take business decisions.

To know the context you need a great understanding of the business beforehand. And you get this great understanding by **asking tons of questions from your client**, browsing the client's website, using all of the sites features and not by diving into GA reports.

> *80% of your analytics problems are solved even before you look into your first GA report once you have developed that great understanding.*

Once you get the right context, you will interpret the data correctly and you will make good business decisions regardless of data collection, data integration, data sampling and other analytics issues.

Since you already know the context beforehand, if something is not right with your analytics data you will know that immediately. You will say to yourself "this cannot be possible".

For example, if you already know that July is a peak season for your client and still the analytics reports are showing less than average sales then it means something could be wrong with ecommerce tracking or the website itself - maybe page load time has increased?

Similarly, you will not go into panic mode when you see that traffic to the website has gone down drastically despite your tremendous SEO efforts simply because you know beforehand that you have now entered the off peak season and consequently demand for your product has gone down.

In fact you will always be in a better position if you develop your business understanding without using GA reports and then later align your understanding with the insight you get from GA report to determine data discrepancies and other analytics issues.

This is in fact a sure fire way to find any issues with your analytics reports at a glance and conform to Agile Analytics methodologies.

Use at least two analytics tools

If you are using two or more analytics tools to gain insight then your probability of interpreting the data and taking the right business decision increases by several folds.

For example, if Google Analytics reports to you that your sales have increased by 20% in the last month and Omniture reports to you that your sales have increased by 30% in the last month then one thing is certain and that is your sales have actually increased in the last month.

If you choose to use only one analytics tool then you can never be 100% sure about your increase in sales.

If Google Analytics reports to you that your sales have increased by 20% in the last month and Omniture reports to you that your sales have decreased by 30% in the last month then one thing is certain and that is one of the tools is collecting and reporting inaccurate data.

If you choose to use only one analytics tool then you may never be able to find out about such data collection issues.

Note: No two analytics tools report the same website usage data for one website. This is quite common and normal. So focus on trends instead of the actual numbers.

Always segment your data

No matter how bad your data is, not segmenting it will only make it worse.

Segmentation is the key to successful optimization and taking the right business decisions.

You need to segment the data to its most granular level before you interpret it or take any decision.

This is because in aggregate form you will never truly get the real insight.

For example, the goal conversion rate of a website can be very misleading because it takes into account every visit that happened on your website from all over the world. Not every visit can lead to a conversion and certainly not the visits from geographical locations which are not your target market.

So in order to get a better insight you need to segment your goal conversion rate. Talk about the goal conversion rate of the branded organic search traffic in your target market area (for example, London) and then take decisions on the basis of such insight.

Get your maths and statistics right

Google Analytics reports are full of averages and if you do not know how averages work then you can easily misinterpret them and get below average or even poor insight.

One of the most misunderstood ratio metrics is conversion rate.

Because of poor statistics skills, many marketers have no idea that conversion rate can negatively correlate with sales and profit.

They think that the conversion rate always positively correlates with conversions i.e. as conversion rate increases, sales always increases and so does profit. But this is not true.

You cannot double your sales just by doubling your marketing budget. It does not work that way.

If the conversion rate of campaign A is 10% and the conversion rate of campaign B is 20%, then it does not always mean that campaign B is performing better than campaign A. You first need to make sure that the difference in conversion rates is statistical significant before you can make any decision.

Similarly, when your website conversion rate jumps from 10% to 12% then it is not necessarily a 2% rise in conversion rate.

You all know this by now, but it is important to reiterate.

A poor understanding of maths and statistics is a sure fire way to fail in any analysis even with the most accurate data in hand.

No matter how good or bad your analytics data is, not using the correct maths and statistics will always make it worse.

Look at the big picture and not the raw numbers

GA data is not very accurate and its metrics could be 10 to 80% off the mark depending upon your traffic size and data sampling issues.

You can easily change the value of almost any metric by just changing your data sample size. You also know that no two analytics tools report the same website usage data even for same website.

Because of these limitations, it is not wise to rely on raw numbers or any single metric for data interpretation. You need to focus on the bigger picture and that is the **trend**.

Measure the performance of your campaigns at the product or page level instead of the keyword level. Do not get bogged down in minute details:

> *"Oh! GA is reporting 300 visits but Omniture is reporting only 210 visits. Look! This keyword generated $200, but last time it generated $500."*

Such types of analysis will just keep you busy in focusing on the 80% that does not really matter instead of the 20% that really matters. Yes I am talking about the mighty 80/20 rule here.

> *80% of your output comes from 20% of your input.*

> *80% of your sales come from 20% of the products.*

So you need to find that 20% and just work on it relentlessly.

Make faith based decisions

Data driven marketers do not make faith based decisions. Now the problem is while they avoid making such decisions, their clients/employers, a.k.a. the entrepreneurs, make such decisions all the time and you cannot really stop them from making such decisions.

Why? Because they know that they will **fail in business** if they stop making faith based decisions. Let me give you one example:

I left my well paid job to start a tech start up. Knowing that 90% of all tech start-ups fail, I should not have even considered taking such action based on data. What if my business failed? What if I cannot pay the bills? What if I never get a job ever again?

But I had to overcome all of these fears and take the **leap of faith.** So I did what I had to. Nothing really bad happened. I have been a happy independent consultant for years now.

Had I been data driven, that 90% failure rate would have stopped me at the very start from taking any action. I would have never become independent and I would still be working somewhere 9-5 and commuting five hours a day.

Likewise, you often hear stories like 'how to quit your job, move to paradise and get paid to change the world' about people who quit their job, sell everything, move to a foreign country and live their **dream life**.

How are they able to do all that? They are able to do that because they take a **leap of faith**.

My friend Danny Dover (a well-known SEO and author of the book 'SEO Secrets') quit his **six figure salary job** to complete his bucket list and is now living a happy and fulfilling life. He travels all over the world throughout the year. For him the word 'holiday' actually means coming back home.

How is he able to do all that? He is able to do all that because he took a **leap of faith**.

> *A leap of faith, in its most commonly used meaning, is the act of believing in or accepting something intangible or unprovable, or without empirical evidence.*
> *Source:* https://en.wikipedia.org/wiki/Leap_of_faith

These people do not pursue their dreams on the basis of likelihood of success or failure. They do not go round looking for facts or research for market statistics to make sure that they are making the right decision. They just go ahead and do it. They do what they believe in and what make them happy, no matter how crazy it may sound to others.

Faith based decisions are an important part of our lives.

All major business decisions are **largely** faith based, from hiring an employee, entering into a business partnership to acquiring a business.

All major life decisions are faith based whether it is friendship, marriage or having kids. You can never venture into the unknown and be innovative and think outside the box if you cannot make decisions without data/facts.

So, why am I telling you all this, in this book on maths and statistics which is supposed to be data driven?

I am presenting you the other side of the decision making process. If you are not an entrepreneur then you need to start thinking like one. Understand their thought process.

You need to understand why sometimes they reject your recommendations even when they are backed up with solid data.

You need to understand why sometimes they reject your whole analysis (no matter how accurate it may seem) and prefer making faith based business decisions and following their gut instinct.

Takeaways

1. Do not automatically dismiss any claim just because it cannot be backed up with data.

2. Understand that the data and tools available to you do not provide complete insight. They are there to help you, not to dissuade you from reality.

3. Understand businesses exist outside of the digital realm and your data collection tools.

4. Know what your analytics tools and KPIs cannot do, as well as what they can. Learn where and when the trade-off should be.

5. Understand that faith-based decisions are necessary for the survival of a business.

6. Think like an entrepreneur and look at things from their perspectives.

Look at the accuracy and credibility of the data source

It is not very hard to fabricate meaningless numbers that tell a story you want people to believe.

The government does that all the time. For example, consider this statement: Obamacare will increase health spending by $7,450 for a typical family of four.

Where does this figure of $7,450 come from? How do you define a typical family? What is the criteria? How reliable is this number?

According to a BBC article 'How bad are US debt levels?' the US has a total debt of almost $17 trillion which is expected to rise to almost $23 trillion in the next five years. Where did this figure of 17 trillion come from? What is the data source and how reliable it is?

Dig deep and you will find it is largely an assumption.

There is even a US debt clock to scare people with big numbers.

Although this debt clock does mention a data source, it does not exactly tell you where these big numbers are being pulled from and how reliable they are? Can you really believe these numbers?

The majority of news out there which talks in numbers has little to no credibility because:

1. They do not mention their data source.
2. They do not mention their data collection methodology.
3. Their data source has little to no credibility.
4. Their data source is outdated and no longer applicable.

The media talk in numbers because numbers generate credibility and people are less suspicious of a statistical claim than they would be of a descriptive argument. For example:

"75% of undergraduates are unemployed."
"The majority of undergraduates are unemployed."

Which statement seems more believable? Obviously the one with numbers.

Throwing some numbers in here and there makes a story look more scientific and well researched. After all who is going to bother to check the data source or the data collection methodology?

Takeaways

1. Beware of meaningless fabricated numbers. They are everywhere.

2. Always look for the data source.

3. Always check the credibility of the data source.

4. Determine how the data has been collected.

5. Determine how current the data source is.

6. Look at lot of different data sources. Do not rely on just one data source.

Always present data with context

If I say to you that my website conversion rate is 15%, does it tell you anything meaningful about the site performance? No.

You do not know whether 15% is a good or bad conversion rate. You do not know whether the conversion rate has increased or decreased in comparison to last month. You do not know whether this conversion rate is the goal conversion rate or the ecommerce conversion rate.

You have no idea whether the reported conversion rate is in aggregated form or segmented.

In other words you are not aware of the context.

Without context, data is meaningless. Comparison adds context to data and make it more meaningful.

If you want to measure the performance of your marketing campaign then you need to compare its performance with the last month's performance. Without such a comparison you will never know whether or not you are making progress.

Consequently, the following report is not very useful:

	Conversion Rate	Orders
Jan	4.56%	2045

You can make this report more useful by comparing it with the last month's performance.

	Conversion Rate	Orders
Jan	4.56%	2045
Dec	4.23%	1945

Takeaways

1. Beware of data which has been presented without context. It is always open to misinterpretation.

2. Comparison adds context to data and make it more meaningful.

3. A standalone metric does not tell you anything meaningful.

Lesson 23: Making the switch from data driven to data smart marketing

Don't get me wrong, there is nothing wrong with being data driven. It is still better than making all business decisions purely on faith or whatever your boss/client has to say.

> *Being data driven is just not good enough. You have to be **data smart**.*

Data driven marketing is all the rage these days. But just like conversion rate optimization, it badly needs an upgrade. In the case of conversion rate optimization, the upgrade was 'conversion optimization' (yes, CRO without conversion rate**)**.

The upgrade for data driven marketing is **data smart marketing** (or smart data marketing, whatever you prefer).

> *When we say or do data smart marketing, our actions and decisions are not purely data driven.*

We do not just blindly follow whatever a metric (like conversion rate) has to say or whatever a chart or report has to say.

We look beyond data and make business decisions based on:

1. Context (extremely important factor often overlooked in data driven marketing).
2. Collective know-how of the organization and industry.
3. All business and marketing activities which are outside the digital realm.

4. Best practices of data analysis, interpretation and statistics.

Data driven marketers tend not to look beyond data. They often disregard any claim which cannot be backed up with data. They often work with the belief that the data and tools available to them somehow provide a complete insight and if something cannot be collected and measured then it should not be taken into account while making important business decisions and calculating the business bottom-line.

When the data is improperly used, we tend to make poor business decisions and that too with lot of confidence.

Data smart marketers on the other hand use **smart data** to make business and marketing decisions.

Smart data is simply data which is used in a smart and intelligent manner.

There is nothing special about this data in itself except it is used intelligently.

When we use smart data we take context into account, we take data collection issues into account and we follow the best practices of data analysis, data interpretation and statistics.

Data smart marketers know what their analytics tools and KPIs cannot do as well as what they can do and where the trade-off should be. They know when and how to make faith-based decisions.

Do not be data blind

"Not everything that counts can be counted, and not everything that can be counted counts." – Albert Einstein

Many marketers/analysts draw conclusions based on the data and tools available to them. How can I be so sure about that? Because I often hear them asking the question **"do you have data to back up this claim?"**

While it is not bad to be data driven, it is worse to be data blind.

Data blindness occurs when someone cannot see anything beyond the data available to him/her.

When you make all of your business and marketing decisions based on the data and tools available to you, you are doing so with the belief that they provide complete insight.

Here is the problem:

All of the data and tools available to you stop working outside the digital realm.

For example, a speaking gig in an industry conference can generate a lot of leads for your business (in the short term or long term) but this is something which you cannot measure through your analytics tools. You do not have any data to back up this claim.

But just because you do not have any data to back up the effectiveness of the speaking gig, it does not mean that it is a useless marketing activity. The same goes for social media campaigns.

The majority of analytics tools are only good in measuring the short term impact of a marketing activity i.e. someone visited the website from a social medium and made a purchase within 30 to 90 days. They fall flat on their face when it comes to measuring the long term impact.

For example, let's imagine your analytics software is constantly telling you that Facebook campaigns are not generating any sales or they are not assisting in any conversions so you should stop the campaigns and move on.

But what if that Facebook campaign is generating sales and is assisting in conversions in the form of direct traffic.

If you blindly rely on the data and tools available to you, you will not be able to see the complete picture. You will more than likely remain busy looking at the short term picture instead of focusing on long term results.

We have a tendency to measure what is easy to measure and ignore all other factors which cannot be measured but which still impact the business bottom-line.

We have a tendency to blindly rely on one or two metrics like conversion rate and statistical significance instead of looking at the big picture in order to define success and failure.

For example, it is not hard to increase your website conversion rate in few seconds. All you have to do is pause all of your paid marketing campaigns. But will that generate more sales for your business? The answer is no.

What will generate more sales is; an increase in average order value and/or ecommerce transactions.

Similarly, we have the tendency to declare the success and failure of an A/B test based on statistical significance results alone. But just because a result is statistically significant, does not always mean that it is practically meaningful.

> *Statistical significance will only tell you whether something works or not. It is not going to tell you how well it works in a range of contexts.*

One of the biggest drawbacks of statistical significance is that it conflates effect size and sample size. Because of this it cannot accurately quantify the size of the difference between two groups (i.e. experimental and control groups).

For that you need to calculate and rely on the effect size (or size of the effect).

Because of all of these implications, whatever you do under conversion optimization must dramatically increase conversion volume (sales, leads). An increase in conversion rate is secondary and should not be your primary target.

This is yet another reason why I never say or do conversion rate optimization. We are not here to optimize the conversion rate. We are here to increase sales and decrease acquisition cost.

> *Not knowing how to use data/metrics effectively is also a type of data blindness. When data is not used intelligently it can result in taking bad decisions with high confidence.*

Develop that great understanding, the rest will take care of itself

The cornerstone of every successful analysis is 'moving in the right direction'. The direction in which your analysis moves will determine the direction in which your marketing campaigns, and eventually your company, will move in order to get the highest possible return on investment.

In order to get the right direction, you have to acquire a great understanding of your client's business, industry, target market, competition and business objectives.

If you do not have that great understanding before you start analysing and interpreting data, you my friend are already moving in the wrong direction. This is the direction which will almost always ensure you return sub optimal results for your company.

Needless to say, a great understanding of a business triumphs over every other metric known to mankind, including our favourite conversion rate. This great understanding is what separates data driven marketers from data smart marketers.

Once you are data smart, you automatically know what data needs to be tracked and when, what to look at, what to overlook and where to look in any analytics reports. You will get a clear sense of what your analytics tools and KPIs can do, what they cannot do and where the trade-off should be.